Grades K-3

Back to School

EVERYTHING YOU NEED TO START YOUR YEAR OFF RIGHT

Contributing Writers
Jan Bates, Trisha Callella, Kim Cernek, Rosa Drew, Debbie Fortunato,
Sandi Hill, Kim Jordano, Deanna Kasch, Jennifer MacLowry, Debbie Martinez,
Tiffani Mugurussa, Denise Skomer

Editor
Alaska Hults

Illustrator
Jane Yamada

Cover Illustrator
Raquel Herrera

Designer
Marek/Janci Design

Cover Designer
Moonhee Pak

Art Director
Tom Cochrane

Project Director
Carolea Williams

Table of Contents

Go!

Introduction

Back to School provides beginning and experienced teachers with practical advice and classroom-tested ideas that are guaranteed to spark student excitement and interest at the start of a new school year. The advice and ideas in this book help you organize your classroom to make everyday tasks less time-consuming, freeing up more of your time to engage your class in fun yet effective lessons. *Back to School* is arranged in three sections:

On Your Mark: Organizational ideas and activities that can be implemented at any time.

Get Set: Ideas and advice for the days leading up to the first day of school.

Go!: Information for the first day and first weeks of school, including how to host and what to include in an effective and informative Back-to-School Night.

You will occasionally find different methods that accomplish the same goal (e.g., Pull Cards from Pockets, page 67, and Build a Rainbow, page 68) to accommodate varying teaching styles and philosophies. Choose the techniques that are comfortable and helpful to you, or use the ideas to help you brainstorm a unique system that will meet your individual needs and resources.

School facilities also differ, especially from region to region. Check with your principal or custodian to approve the use of materials this book suggests, especially when an activity or idea involves putting something in or on a wall, window, or ceiling.

Look for this symbol throughout the book to find shortcuts designed by expert teachers.

This symbol signals tried-and-true information for getting parents involved, keeping them active in the education of their child, and/or maintaining a successful relationship with them.

Dog-ear the pages you want to come back to. Use sticky notes to remember where that fun icebreaker is. Paper-clip the lists of topics to include in your Back-to-School Night. Photocopy the tips on keeping your students on-task, and post them by your desk. Finally, keep this book close at hand. You'll come back to it again and again.

Manage Materials

Many teachers suffer from a lack of adequate storage for the many materials they use. Consequently, materials get lost or are difficult to find when needed. The ideas in this section solve the problem of keeping materials you and your students bring to the classroom in order and accessible. In addition, you'll find helpful advice on what to have on hand at the start of the school year.

Store Bulletin Board Borders

Bulletin board borders are easily ruined, unless they are stored in a box specifically made for borders. Use frosting containers or baby-formula cans to store your borders as an inexpensive, compact alternative. Roll your borders, place them inside the container, snap on the lid, and then tape a short piece of the border to the front of the container to identify which border is inside. These containers stack easily, and the borders will not get wrinkled or torn.

Laminate borders before you use them for added durability and longevity.

Find Individual Browsing Boxes

Collect magazine file boxes or cereal boxes, and photograph each student. Label each box with a student's name, and glue his or her photo above the label. Line the boxes up in alphabetical order within the students' reach so that they can access and return their box. Invite students to

- keep in their box journals and books they are reading during instruction time.

- store unfinished work in the boxes. Have students check their box and get their papers—saving you teaching time, since you do not have to pass them out.

- place completed special projects in the boxes, and then easily collect them in alphabetical order.

Keep the boxes on a shelf rather than in desks or cubbies so that the materials are safe and do not inadvertently get taken home.

Store by Theme

Store your materials by themes to keep everything together. Invest in some cardboard banker's boxes or large plastic storage containers with lids. Keep all of the boxes or containers the same size for easy stacking and storing. Include in each theme box books, videos, puppets, pocket chart materials, bulletin board borders, pictures, black-line masters, and any manipulatives that go with your unit. Once your box is complete, make a list of the items in the box. Laminate the list, and tape it to the front of the box. Even items that are used for several themes will be easy to find.

 Hang a laminated, lined chart near the classroom door. Use string to attach a washable marker to it. When you invite students to take items home, have them write their name and the item they are borrowing on the chart. When students return the items, have them wipe off their name and item.

Organize Student Supplies

Help students learn to organize and keep track of their supplies with these ideas:

For Individual Students

■ Obtain a small plastic storage box or shoe box for each student. Place an adhesive label on the outside of each box with the student's name on it. (If you use student numbers, write the number so labels can be reused each year.) Next, have students fill their box with their supplies (e.g., pencils, crayons, scissors, erasers). Keep the boxes on a shelf alphabetized by student name. Encourage students to go to their box and get supplies as needed. Reuse the boxes each year, replacing the labels as needed.

■ Collect large, wide aluminum cans (e.g., 1-quart vegetable cans). Cut off the lids, and sand the inside so that there are no sharp edges. Hot-glue felt or fabric to the bottom of the cans to keep them quiet against desk-tops and tabletops. Leave the labels in place, and invite students to glue scraps of wallpaper or fabric to the labels. Have students fill the decorated cans with their supplies.

For a Group

■ Place small, inexpensive flowerpots at each student table or desk cluster. Fill the pots with markers, pencils, pens, and other supplies students may need during the school day.

■ Hang three-tiered baskets (commonly used to hold vegetables) from the ceiling over each student grouping. Use extra chain or rope to ensure students can reach the baskets. Fill the baskets with supplies for students to share.

■ Provide each table grouping with a plastic lazy Susan or a rotating cake base. Attach paper cups to the top with rubber cement. Fill each cup with school tools, such as glue, scissors, crayons, markers, pens, and pencils. Place a tool caddy in the center of each table.

Collect Garbage

Place small garbage pails, sand pails, brown paper bags, or plastic baskets on classroom tables to collect all paper scraps and other trash. Have students place their trash in these containers rather than clutter the tables or push scraps to the floor. This minimizes mess, as well as the need for students to get up frequently to throw away their paper scraps. Have students empty the containers into a larger trash can.

Establish a "Community Use Policy" for sharing classroom materials. Include rules for treating materials with care, sharing items, and returning tools to their proper places after use. Display the policy, and review the procedures frequently.

Organize Your Desk

You may not spend much time at your desk, but you will need to visit it to get at the key items it contains. If you can choose your desk, pick one that has several drawers. Set up at least one drawer for hanging files. Consider keeping the following supplies and decorative accents at your desk:

On Top of Desk	Inside Desk
calendar	large, black chart markers
family photo	fine-line felt-tip markers
hole punch	drawer organizers
paper-clip holder	large and small envelopes
paper clips (large and small)	hanging file folders
pencils	ink pens
pencil holder	permanent markers
scissors (at least 3 pairs)	rubber bands
small plant	ruler
stacking baskets or trays	sticky notes
stapler	several kinds of notepads
tape dispenser	staple remover
	thank-you notes

Keep the items you will use most in your top drawer. Arrange the rest of the items in the drawers in order of necessity. If your desk has a drawer for hanging files, use the files for important school-related materials or for student portfolios. Label folders so you can find them quickly.

Place an in-basket on your desk for mail and notes from parents or the office. Put items in the basket as you receive them, and then go through the basket at the end of each day. The less you have on the top of your desk the better. A family photo and a small plant are enough decorative accents. Too many items makes your desk appear cluttered and unorganized.

 Another way to organize your "teaching tools" is to place them in a clear-pocket shoe organizer hung by your desk. This helps you see everything at a glance and locate items quickly.

Organize Overhead Projector Materials

Here are a few simple tricks to help you organize overhead projector markers, manipulatives, and transparencies:

- Glue magnets to the side of a small cardboard box—empty crayon boxes work well. Fill the box with overhead markers, and attach the box to the side of the overhead projector or the cart on which it sits.

- Tie a small apron decorated with fabric paints, buttons, and glitter glue around the top of the projector cart or the base of the projector. Fill the pockets with markers and the clear math manipulatives you use often.

- When presenting a lesson with several overhead transparencies, place a small sticky note on the edge of each transparency.

Number the sticky notes in the order they will be used, and write an identifying code word or phrase to help you recognize each page. You will be able to easily identify which transparency comes next in your lesson without losing valuable time shuffling through pages to find the one you need.

Keep Track of Chalk and Dry-Erase Markers

Many classroom chalkboards and large dry-erase boards are magnetized. Obtain inexpensive storage containers equipped with magnetic strips, or make your own by gluing magnets to small boxes. Use these containers to store your chalk right on the board. Store dry-erase markers with the tip down to keep them from drying out. Find a lightweight cup (even a decorated sturdy paper cup will do), hot-glue a magnetic strip to the side, and use that to store your markers. If you use a lot of markers, pin the cup to the bulletin board or wall next to your board.

Do not cover or place objects in front of the vents on an overhead projector. Some projectors will shut off automatically when they get too hot.

Organize Paint Supplies

Having students paint in the classroom can be messy. To alleviate some of this mess, try the following:

- Use paper cups for paint, and throw them away when finished.

- Line paint cups with plastic sandwich bags. When students are finished, throw out the bags and keep the clean cups.

- Use frosting containers for paint cups. Snap the lid on when students are finished painting to keep the paint from drying.

Be Safe!

Use a backpack as an "Emergency Bag," and store it by the door you exit in an emergency. Include the following items:

- first aid kit—disposable gloves, cotton, antiseptic wipes, various sizes of adhesive and elastic bandages stored in a resealable plastic bag.

- class list.

- nametag necklaces. In advance, make a necklace for each student out of yarn or string and an index card. On the index card, include the student's name, allergies, phone number, emergency information, and parent release information.

- dry-erase board and marker.

- pencil, crayons, and paper.

In an emergency, grab the bag and have the class exit immediately. At your designated area, take role by distributing the necklaces. Any leftover necklaces will tell you who is missing. Put the leftover necklaces around your neck so you remember who the missing (or absent) students are. If you must wait before returning to your classroom, keep students occupied by playing games with your class on the dry-erase board. Or, in the event of an actual emergency, write key information on the board to display to other adults without having to yell. The pencil, crayons, and paper are for emergency notes and for students to use while waiting. In the event of an actual emergency, check students off the class list when they are picked up by their parents.

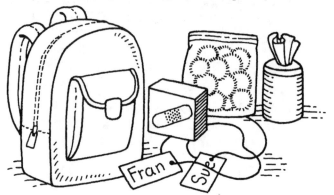

 Collect men's button-down shirts to use as paint smocks. Cut or roll up sleeves, and use binder clips to make a snug fit around students' wrists. Find the shirts at thrift stores and garage sales, or ask for the shirts in your class newsletter or wish list.

Manage Time

Even the most experienced teacher may find that there are simply not enough hours in the day. The following ideas and activities will help you organize your schedule and set up a terrific support system of willing and able parent volunteers.

Create a Daily Schedule

Write out a schedule for each day of the week on the Daily Schedule reproducible (page 92). Attach a copy to your daily lesson-plan book. Give a copy to the office, and share a copy with parents at Back-to-School Night. Encourage parents not to schedule necessary medical appointments during core-curriculum lessons. Keep the following tips in mind:

- When planning your day, try to integrate the curriculum as much as possible to make learning meaningful.

- Include district allotments and routines set in the school schedule, such as lunch, recess, and any regularly occurring activities or events (e.g., music, art). Try to have long, uninterrupted blocks of time for language arts.

- Plan time each day for students to independently read books of their choice. This is a great cool-down activity after a break such as recess.

- Try different schedules from year to year until you find one that works for you and your students. However, if a schedule is not working, change it! Be as consistent as possible. Students need the routine.

If you are new to teaching, find a colleague who can lead you through the year. Find someone who can pass on any need-to-know information about your school—including answers to essential questions. Find someone who will give you room to grow, but speak up if he or she sees you having a problem. This will save you countless hours in the long run.

Delegate Work to Parent Volunteers

Most parents want to be involved and are a great resource for making classroom life easier and better for all. Parents who work in the classroom will spread the word about all the hard work you do. By taking care of the more time-consuming daily-grind tasks (see the list below), they free up your time to run independent-learning centers, work individually with students, read journals, and do authentic assessment. Here are just a few of the jobs you can give parent volunteers:

Classroom Help
Read with students
Check homework
Write dictated stories
Work with individual students
Tear down and put up bulletin boards
Assist students with computers

Home Help
Assemble books
Trim laminated materials
Calculate book order
Word process
Make modeling dough

Timesaving Jobs
Organize room volunteers
Manage phone chain
Communicate special needs to parents
Organize committees

Workroom Help
Make die cuts
Cut paper
Bind books
Publish newsletter or class books (e.g., word processing, binding)

Tell parents that studies show parent participation to be a top indicator of student success.

Motivate Parents to Volunteer

Tell parents in your newsletters, in person, and at Back-to-School Night about

- connecting home and school. Volunteering gives parents a proactive opportunity to affect their child's education.

- influencing students positively. Many students perform better in school when they know their parents care and are watching.

- opening lines of communication. Volunteering helps parents have more informed conversations with their children and the teacher about what goes on in the classroom.

- creating their own feeling of success. They'll get the opportunity to be a contributing member of the classroom community.

- joining the group of supportive interested parent volunteers. They have the opportunity to make friends with the other volunteers.

- gaining insight into their child's education. They'll learn how to work with their own children to help them do well in school and improve their children's skills.

Invite Parents to Work at Home

Many parents want to help, but cannot come into the classroom because they work or have other children at home. To help parents get involved, set up a parent work box. Write *Parent Take-Home Work* on several large manila envelopes, and laminate them. Number the envelopes to keep track of them and their contents. Place a clipboard inside the box with the envelopes and a numbered sign-out sheet. Invite parents to sign out an envelope on the clipboard. Be sure to include directions and a sample of what you want done. Include a due date to ensure you get the material back on time.

 Tell parents that any time they can contribute is valuable, whether it's one hour a day, one hour a week, or one hour a month. This tells them that you respect their time. For only one day a week, some parents can make arrangements at their job to come in an hour later.

Host a Volunteer Training Night

Set up a time to meet with your volunteers before they begin working in your classroom. Just as you set standards for students in your classroom, set standards for your parent volunteers. Explain your class discipline plan, and use the Volunteer Guidelines reproducible (page 93) or create your own to help parents understand your expectations. Ask parents to keep student information confidential. Demonstrate how to use equipment they may need, including office equipment. Take time to answer questions, and tell them they can talk to you about any problems that may come up in the future. Do tell them that their classroom visit is not the time to discuss their child, however. Be sure to tell parents your feelings about bringing other children into the classroom with them.

Show Your Appreciation

Above all, make sure your volunteers feel valued. Try these ideas:

- On holidays or special occasions, have each student make a page for a special book or card for each parent volunteer.

- Put together thank-you treat bags on days when your volunteers will not expect it. Give one to each parent during a particular week. Try giving volunteers

  - a bag of Hershey's® Kisses™ and Hugs™ with a short note of thanks. Attach a note that says *You are a Lifesaver!* to a pack of Lifesavers™. Attach a note that says *You bring a Bit-O-Honey to our room! Thanks!* to a Bit-O-Honey candy bar.

  - a thank-you note cut up like a puzzle.

  - a class photo signed by each student.

- If you notice that a parent looks uncomfortable with a chosen task, give him or her other options for volunteering.

- In your morning messages, include the name of the volunteer visiting that day. For example, *Today is Monday, February 12. We are so lucky to have Mrs. Phillips helping us today. For lunch we will eat hamburgers. After lunch, we will take our math test.*

 Invite parents to sign up as substitute volunteers in case of another parent's absence. With permission, collect the volunteers' phone numbers and distribute them at your training night. Ask parents to call for a sub when they are unable to come to the classroom.

Have a Master Plan

Take the time to plan the year—where you are going, how you are going to get there, and how everything is linked together. Make a chart on the inside of a legal-size file folder that has a column for each month you teach and a row for each curriculum area. Save a column for "Other." Label each box by month, and then write in the themes that you know you will teach. Then, take a look at your curriculum.

What are your big math, science, and social studies units? When is state testing? Write those in. What field trips are you planning? Make field-trip reservations now because if you wait until January to reserve your Valentine's Day tour of the chocolate factory, you'll find yourself stuck with the 2 p.m.-on-Friday-meltdown tour (the kids, not the chocolate).

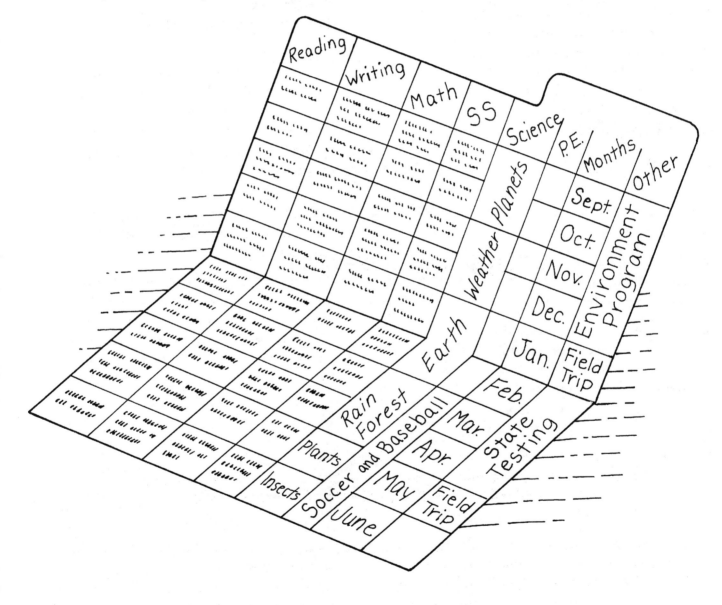

 Label a plastic tub *Help!* so volunteers can check to see what you need done without interrupting your instruction. Place written directions and all necessary materials in large resealable plastic bags. Place the bags inside the tub with a sample of the finished product.

Manage Paper

Even before school begins paperwork can pile up. Try these simple ideas to prepare your classroom for the start of the school year and to keep important forms and information in order at your fingertips.

Organize Important Information

Organize in a three-ring binder important information, such as class rules and procedures, permission slips, or information for new students. Use clear sheet protectors to store the original copy in, and use pocket folders behind the original to store photocopies. When you receive a new student or a parent requests a copy of a form, you will have the information easily available.

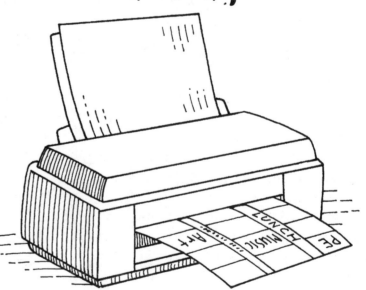

Make Lesson Plans Easy

Use a computer to make a lesson plan template, including elements of the schedule that do not change (e.g., lunchtime, recess, P. E.). Make two-sided copies, and use a three-hole punch to ready them for a binder. You'll only need to make minor changes from year to year.

To save time, prepare templates for calendars, journals, reading logs, or other teacher-made materials ahead of time. Prepare your masters for each month or unit needed, and then photocopy a class set plus a few extras in the event that a new student joins your class mid-month or unit. File the copies in hanging file folders so they will be ready for you.

Use Survival Lists

Use the Lists reproducible (page 94) to list and mark off tasks as you complete them. Use the *Survival List* on the reproducible, or give the blank list your own title. Lists might include *Materials I Need to Label, Papers I Need to Copy, Items to Give to the Office,* and *Questions I Need Answered.* At the end of each day, you will be able to look back over the day with a sense of accomplishment. Your time will be spent more wisely because a list will keep you focused.

Collect Student Work

Write each student's name on a three-ring divider tab, and put the dividers in a three-ring binder in alphabetical order. Place assessments, student writing samples, spelling tests, math samples, and other critical work in this notebook. At parent/teacher conferences, all you need to do is flip to that student's name and review the collected samples. When the next parent arrives, you are ready to flip to the next student and share his or her work.

Also, when preparing report cards, it is easier to bring a notebook home than a stack of file folders.

 Encourage Book Orders

Make photocopies of the Book Order Parent Letter (page 95), and keep the copies in a file folder. Every month, skim through the book-order form and list on the letter three good book choices with a brief description of why they would make a good addition to each student's home bookshelf. Fill in the appropriate dates and book-order information on the letter, make a copy for each student, have a volunteer staple each letter to a book-order form, and send the form and letter home with students.

Parents will appreciate the time you save them and more of your students will order good books.

Put the class list on a clipboard for each subject. Use the clipboard to evaluate work on the spot, especially cooperative learning.

17

Manage Centers

Before school starts, you will need to set up learning centers and resource areas (e.g., computer centers and reading areas). A well-designed center can help students focus and stay on track. For more ideas on managing students, see Establish Procedures and Routines (pages 56–65) and Foster On-Target Behavior (pages 66–74).

Schedule Groups at Centers

Assign students to groups, and give each group a color. (For more on grouping, see page 61.) Make a large and small circle from tagboard, and divide both circles into equal sections. Color each section of the small circle the same color as a group. Attach it to the center of the large circle with a brass fastener. Place a picture in each section of the large circle to represent each center. Turn the wheel whenever groups are to move to a new center.

Create Center Signs

If you have specific center areas, center signs are a great way to designate the areas. Try these ways to display your signs:

- Attach center signs to long pieces of yarn, and hang one above each center. This keeps the signs off the work surface and out of the way. Be sure to hang the signs high enough for adults to walk under, but low enough for everyone to read them.

- Place your center signs in clear acrylic photo frames. On one side, display the name of the center, and on the other, display the directions for the center activity.

Store Listening Center Materials

Use manila envelopes or resealable plastic bags and a box or large plastic basket to store books and cassettes for your listening center. Place each set of books and cassette in a separate envelope or bag. Use a permanent marker to label the envelopes or bags, and place them in the box or basket. Place cardboard after every three sets of books to keep them from slouching over. Label the tops of the cardboard if you plan to separate your books by themes.

Organize the Class Library

Keeping the classroom library tidy can be a challenge, but with a few simple storage containers, organizing all those books can be easy. Invest in several plastic dishpans, large plastic baskets, or storage containers. You will also need alphabet decals and small dot stickers. Separate all your books. Separate them alphabetically or organize them by themes (e.g., poetry, fairy tales, alphabet, numbers). Once you have separated them, use the dots to color-code each theme or group of books by placing the same colored dot on each book in a group. Next, place the books in the containers, and label the containers using the alphabet decals (or label and tape sentence strips to the containers) and a matching colored dot. Have students return books to the container with the same colored dot. Research shows students often make book choices by looking at the cover illustration rather than the title on the spine of the book. The containers allow students to see the cover of the book, rather than just the spine.

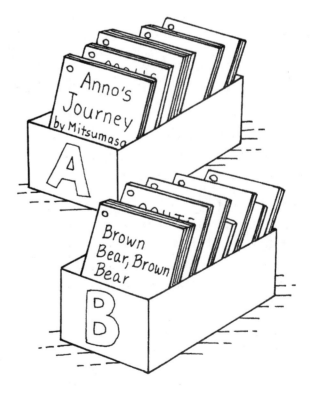

Create a Reading Corner

Use your library bookshelves to create an enclosed reading corner. Instead of stacking books, display them so that students are able to see the front covers of the books. In addition, try a few of the following suggestions to make your reading corner attractive to students:

■ Include beanbags, pillows with washable covers, and a couch for comfort.

■ Include a lamp for focused light and the warmth of a filament bulb.

■ Create barriers from the rest of the room with bookcases, cinder blocks and wood planks, or a quilt or fabric hung from a chart rack.

■ Sort the books by genre.

■ Include books ranging from kindergarten through fifth-grade reading level.

 Use points you earn from book-order clubs to purchase books for your class library, extra copies of your read-aloud books (for students who want to read along with you), and books for a take-home reading program (see page 65).

Manage the Computer Center

Computers are excellent educational tools. They motivate students and can help them develop their problem-solving skills. However, they come with their own little bag of management problems, so here are some tricks to keep your computer-time routine on track:

- Use a kitchen timer to keep track of student time on the computer.

- Place a hanging file box next to the computer. Give each student a hanging folder labeled with his or her name. Keep student disks, worksheets, time logs, and other important computer papers in this folder. Students will be less likely to misplace this important information if it is always left near the computer station.

- Locate the computer near a bulletin board (away from a sink or magnets). Use the bulletin board to highlight assignments, note new software choices, and identify any key combination functions that students may have trouble remembering.

- Establish computer rules. Cover the proper care and use of the computer hardware and software. Familiarize yourself with your district's Internet policy, and explain it to your students and their parents. Print the rules and the consequences of breaking them on a contract, and distribute one to every student. Discuss the rules and consequences with students, and have them take the contract home to read and discuss with their parents. Ask both students and parents to sign the contract. Keep the contracts in students' computer folders.

- Train a group of students to be computer experts. When a student on the computer needs help, one of your experts can help solve the problem.

- If your students will be doing a lot of word processing and publishing, give each student his or her own disk. This will protect students' precious work from being accidentally deleted from the computer hard drive or from other unforeseen accidents. Follow these simple steps:

  1. Buy preformatted disks for your computer type.

  2. Place each disk one at a time into the disk drive.

  3. Label the disk with the student's name as prompted by your computer.

  4. Remove the disk, and place on it a disk label with the student's name.

  5. Keep the disks in a disk box next to the computer.

  When students need to work on the computer, have them save their work to their own disk. At the end of the school year, pass the disks on to next year's teacher or erase, rename, and relabel them for next year's students.

- Keep a computer log near the computer. As students finish working, have them record the disk they used or the assignments they completed. This log will remind students where they were during their last computer session. It also reflects student progress and can be used as an assessment tool.

- Ask for computer-savvy parent volunteers to work with students on a weekly basis. These volunteers can provide one-on-one assistance for students and free you to work with other students.

- Once a week present a new computer skill to students. Such skills include saving a document, printing a document, and opening a file. Demonstrate the skill, give students time to practice the skill, and then have them write about what they learned. Ask students to keep these technical journals in their computer folder so they can refer to them when working independently.

Computer Log

Name	File	Progress
Carla	Elephants	Finished TOC
Raul	Circus	Finished page one
Lester	Rodeo	halfway through second page
Jaime	Space	Ready to print

Create a Learning Environment

When you open a child's heart, you open a child's mind. One way to do this is to provide your students with an environment that makes them feel safe, welcome, and focused on learning. The following ideas and advice will help you create a room where you and your students can spend all day learning *and* having fun.

Design a Cozy Classroom

Make your room atmosphere cozy. You want your classroom to feel comfortable and inviting for both you and your students. Try the following ideas to make your room reflect a warm learning environment:

- Line your bulletin boards with fabric. Use fabric with prints that match the seasons or a current theme.

- Add some curtains or valances. If you are a whiz with a sewing machine, stitch a few valances to match the fabric on the bulletin boards.

- Add a couch or small love seat, futons (chairs), or beanbags to your reading area.

- Add lighting such as a small lamp in the reading area next to the couch or chairs.

- Brighten your room with plants. Have a class gardener take care of the plants. Install grow lights (or just buy the grow-light bulbs and install them in any lamp with a porcelain socket) for plants in classrooms with little natural light.

- Ask students what items would help make the room more inviting. Post some of their suggestions on a wish list for parents who are willing to donate some of the items.

 Before you arrange your furniture, draw a map of the room and label each area (e.g., bulletin boards, library area, computer area, dramatic-play area, centers, rug area). This kind of planning helps you avoid moving heavy furniture more than once.

Create a Planter Box

Welcome students and visitors with a planter box full of beautiful flowers right outside your classroom door. Use a large wooden planter box, a wine barrel, or old wooden block boxes found around school. These work well because they have wheels on the bottom. When you are ready to plant, have students help; they love digging in the dirt, and it is a great way to introduce a study of plants.

Keep Cleaning Supplies on Hand

Your school will employ a janitor to keep things clean, so, by and large, this is not your responsibility. Even so, your room reflects your efforts, not the cleaning staff's. Stock up on a few cleaning supplies to keep your classroom sparkling bright, and remember to keep items such as the following out of the sight and reach of students:

- window cleaner

- all-purpose surface cleaner

- paper towels

- adhesive gum remover (for sticky labels on desks or gum on rug)

- sponge mop (for those unexpected spills)

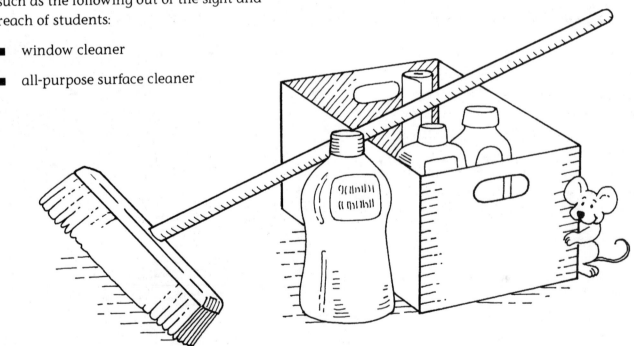

Know Your Butcher Paper

Some teachers cover the entire wall in butcher paper because they like to, and some because water stains or age necessitates it. Before you cover large areas with butcher paper, locate all electrical outlets and light switches to avoid covering them. It does not matter whether you hang butcher paper in horizontal or vertical stripes, but do not cut the paper to the exact size. Cut the paper a little too long and fold the ends under, lining up the sides. This will give you a straight edge without a lot of measuring.

The day you hang butcher paper is a great time to make friends with upper-grade students wandering around the school. Their chatter provides great company, they will help you get the butcher paper to your room, they are helpful in holding the paper in place while you staple, and they issue copious compliments when the work is done. Give your volunteers a small handful of candy and effusive thanks when you are done, and you will have upper-grade student volunteers you can depend on for the rest of the year.

Make Your Own "Star Chair"

Create a "Star Chair" for your students to sit in when the spotlight is on them. Depending on the condition of the chair, you may wish to paint the whole chair or just add some decorative features. Paint *I Am a Star!* on the backrest of the chair. Students will love sharing their writing or experiences while sitting on it.

I Am a Star!

Keep a few baby wipes on hand for quick cleaning. Baby wipes can be used to wipe off students' desks and hands, computer keyboards, and earphones. These handy little wipes are inexpensive, and they smell good, too.

25

Choose Pets for Your Classroom (or Not)

There are pros and cons to having pets in the classroom. Think about what you hope to accomplish with pets, and weigh the costs and benefits carefully. Classroom pets require a great deal of care—even a fish tank requires cleaning. Consider these points before you go shopping:

PROS

■ Pets give students an opportunity to be responsible for and care for another living thing.

■ They make a room cozy and homelike.

■ They can be incorporated into class activities, such as writing workshop or science, to make these activities more meaningful.

CONS

■ Many students have allergies to animals—even small ones.

■ Money for their care and feeding may come out of your pocket.

■ Furry friends require continuous care and cleaning.

■ Care for the animals on weekends and vacations requires management, and the pet is probably yours to take home over a very long break such as summer vacation.

■ A fish tank can stay and be maintained in the classroom, even over a very long break, but can be expensive to set up. Also, fish are like plants in that you either have the knack for keeping them alive or you do not.

Label, Label, Label

Label everything from drawers to boxes to containers. Labeling helps you find things quickly and easily. It also helps parent volunteers and substitutes. Keep these labeling ideas in mind:

- Labels do not have to be fancy. Use regular white labels or masking tape. Use a permanent marker so the ink does not rub off.

- Do not label everything in your classroom before school starts. Plan time on the first day of school for students to help you with this. They will be more responsible when putting things away. Use shared or interactive writing activities to have less fluent writers create labels on sentence strips. Have students who are more fluent writers do their own writing. Laminate the labels before displaying them.

- For those items that you label yourself, glue photos, drawings, or pictures from school supply catalogs on sentence strips and label each illustration. Walk students through the classroom so they know exactly where to place each item.

Communicate with Parents and Students

No one knows your students better than their own parents, and although parents do not always come to you with questions and advice about their children, they may have concerns and opinions. Be proactive and seize every opportunity to open lines of communication with your students' parents. Your students will benefit at home and in your classroom from the partnership you form with their parents. The following ideas, activities, and advice will help make your year go more smoothly and be part of the impact you have on your students' lives.

Send Home Homework Envelopes

Send home your students' class work at the end of every week. Label a 10" x 13" (25.5 cm x 33 cm) manila envelope with each student's first and last name and room number. You may also want to write *Please return every Monday.* Laminating the envelopes will make them last about half of the school year. Tell parents when to expect the envelopes with student work, class newsletters, and other important school-related materials and notes.

 Add motivational and cute stickers to some of your notes to parents. Regardless of age, everyone loves stickers and stars.

Reach Out

The beginning of the year is a perfect opportunity to reach out to parents and build the foundation for a strong classroom community. Experiment with a variety of approaches, such as those listed here, to meet the needs of all your families.

- In advance, prepare necklaces made of small, construction paper cards and yarn. Have the illustration on the necklace reflect whatever theme you are beginning the year with and write *I had a terrific first day!* Send students home with them on the first day.

- Ease student anxieties about starting school by inviting them to visit the classroom before school begins. Invite parents and students to a "Meet the Teacher Tea." Have a few tables set up with coloring supplies or other easy-to-do activities such as pattern blocks. Have another area set up for juice and cookies and a third area for parents to fill out forms you need from them (e.g., medical release forms, get-to-know-you survey).

- Send a welcome postcard to each student before school starts. Tell students you are very excited to meet them and cannot wait for school to begin. Describe some of the beginning-of-the-year curriculum to get them excited.

- Throw a back-to-school potluck for your students and their families the first or second week of school. This is a great way to meet the families of your students and for the families to meet each other. Place a potluck sign-up sheet outside your door, and send home invitations for a night of fun. Remember to invite your family, too.

- Send an invitation before school starts to tell students that your classroom will be fun, as well as a place of learning. Include on the invitation *Who:* (student's name), *What: First Day of School, When:* (date), *Where:* (school name and room number), *Hosted by:* (your name), *Bring:* (themed item), *Why: To Start off a Great Year and Make New Friends.* You may even want to include a photo of yourself and a note about why you are excited about this school year. If you have a room theme, invite each student to bring in a theme-related item to share on the first day (e.g., bear theme—a stuffed bear; rainbow theme—something that is a favorite color; ocean theme—shells). On the first day, have students share their item with the class.

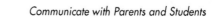

29

 Distribute a Newsletter

Maintain ongoing, upbeat communication with parents through your class newsletter. Send one home at least once a month—once a week, if you can swing it. Start with basic information, and add to it as you get in the habit of sending it home. Here are a few tips to keep in mind:

- Type your newsletter on your computer rather than handwrite it. It will look more professional and will be easier for your parents to read, no matter how perfect your penmanship. *Do not write in letter form—they will not read it.*

- To begin, open a word-processing document and save it as "Class Newsletter." Next, create a catchy title, like *K–1 News, The Room 14 Chronicle,* or *Our Class Gazette.* Make your heading bold, and experiment with different fonts and font sizes. Each week, reopen the same document, change the date, add new items about curriculum, and recap last week's lessons.

- Separate your information into articles. Include titles and short summaries (e.g., *Reading, Writing, Pen Pals, Birthdays, Classroom News, School News, Social Studies, Science, Math*). Create a border around each main section to visually separate sections. This helps parents feel like they have time to read it. Use a clear, easy-to-read font.

- Newsletters need to include the following: praise for the class (find something good to say), curriculum updates, dates to mark on family calendars, tips on how to help at home, and reminders of things students need to bring to school.

 Remember to print thank-you notes for donations in your class newsletters.

- Print out your newsletter, and add a photo of a class activity. Parents will enjoy receiving pictures of what is taking place—even in black and white. Add photocopies of student work on the back. Invite students to nominate a few samples or work alphabetically from your class list, but rotate the work represented (e.g., by theme, by student, by content area). Reduce student work on your copy machine so four to six pieces can fit on a page. Include a brief sentence describing the assignment. Write the student's name by each piece.

- Photocopy a class set of newsletters, and give one to each student. Invite each student to write in his or her own words favorite events and activities from the past week.

- Send home newsletters on the same day each time. Parents will appreciate the routine. Be realistic at the time you have available to commit to publishing your newsletter. Begin with what is reasonable for your schedule and student population.

- As the year progresses, consider having parent volunteers help your students write their own articles. Invite students to tell about classroom events in their own words, and then find a parent volunteer willing to edit the articles with each author. The finished pieces will be easy to type up, and students will hungrily devour their writing and those of their peers.

31

Make a Moveable Announcement Board

When you need to get parents' attention before school or need to display important information, put an easel outside your door. Use clothespins to clip your notices to the easel. Provide a few pens so parents can write messages. Use the easel to

- remind parents about book orders. (Provide a few order forms.)

- remind parents about field trips. (Provide a few permission slips.)

- have parents sign up for parent/teacher conferences, a class potluck, or other events.

Create a Classroom Contact List

Improve communication in your classroom by providing families with each student's address, phone number, and parents' names. A phone list will help you or your parent volunteers contact students' families when you need help on a class project or want to brag about a student's positive attitude. Lifelong friendships are built in the primary grades by parents getting to know each other and their students. Be sure to get permission from parents for each child you place on the list.

# Have a Homework Plan

Before you give students homework, prepare parents for what kind of homework you will be sending home, their role, and the schedule for taking homework home and returning it. Reward students for following your homework plan for the first few weeks, until they get in the routine. Praise parents in your newsletter for helping their children develop responsibility for homework.

Schedule Routine Parent/Teacher Conferences

Many schools have fall parent/teacher conferences in which parents are given the opportunity to discuss the needs of their child(ren) with his or her teacher. These conferences are an opportunity to establish a good rapport with parents, review the child's strengths and weaknesses, and set goals for the future. Choose from these ways to have parents sign up for conferences or establish a schedule:

- Post a conference sign-up sheet at Back-to-School Night.

- Post a conference sign-up sheet outside your classroom door, several days before you send home conference notices.

- Send home a note letting parents know conferences are coming up. Ask them to list three different days and times that they are available to meet with you.

- Assign everyone a time. Send home a note at least a month in advance, notifying parents of their time and inviting them to contact you if they need to change their time.

 Create a bulletin board just for parents. Post information about parenting classes, copies of school or class newsletters, and community information. Invite parents to post information for other parents, such as requests for day care recommendations.

33

Manage Routine Parent/Teacher Conferences

Parents often feel uncomfortable with parent/teacher conferences. Make the conference comfortable for all. Make sure you have enough large chairs. Parents may feel awkward sitting in small student chairs. Offer the parents paper and pen so they may write down information. Begin the conference by telling them you are interested in their child. Ask questions about their child such as

- What are his or her hobbies at home? What does he or she enjoy most about school?

- What are your goals for him or her this school year?

- What do you see as his or her strengths and weaknesses regarding school?

Consider sending the questions home ahead of time for parents to return when they come to the conference. This gives parents time to reflect on their answers and gives them something to take to the meeting. Parents will feel like they are being listened to, and you will gain insight into each student and his or her family. Parents often arrive before their scheduled conference time. Provide a few

chairs and a table in the hallway outside your classroom. Leave copies of current articles that would be helpful for parents to read. Also include copies of reading lists, suggestions for ways to read with their child, and other information you choose to share with parents. This is also a perfect opportunity to display class books, student projects, computer slide shows, and artwork.

Use a Parent Contact Sheet

Use the Contact reproducible (page 96) to document communication with your students' families. If you make a phone call, send a note home with a student, mail a letter, or have a spontaneous meeting with a student's parents,

record notes about the conversation or contents of the note or letter on the sheet. This will save confusion later when you try to recall any agreements made on behalf of the student.

Call a Parent/Teacher Conference to Settle Concerns

You may occasionally need to call an emergency parent/teacher conference. Establishing and maintaining open communication with parents is essential for meeting your students' needs. Parent/teacher conferences help you achieve this goal.

Do the following before the meeting:

- Prepare notes about the student. Include observations of the student's strengths and areas of concern. Do not write anything about a student that you do not want a parent to read. Leave a section on the page to take notes during the conference. At the bottom of the page, indicate what actions you will take based on the information discussed in the conference (e.g., you will send home a weekly progress report about the student's work habits). Review these pages after the conference, and keep them on file for future reference.

- Prepare a student work folder to share with parents during the conference. This will serve as documentation to support your observations of the student. If behavior is an issue, include documentation to show the frequency of the behavior. Student work, test data, and anecdotal information are also useful.

Parents are their child's best advocate. Develop a trusting relationship with parents. Listen to their observations and concerns. Their insights may provide critical data that will be useful in meeting students' needs.

A difficult conference may be emotional for both parents and teacher. Remain calm and professional in all situations. Initially, some parents may react defensively to concerns about their child's behavior or performance. Keep the best interests of the child as the constant focus of the meeting to disarm any negative feelings—yours or theirs. Occasionally, parents may need a day or two to reflect on the conference before they are willing to take steps you suggest. Make it clear to them that they have time to consider your suggestions. Continue to communicate a sincere interest in their child's well-being to reach an understanding that works for the parents, the child, and you.

What We Know	Goals	Actions

Occasionally, a conference may involve other professionals (e.g., a social worker, a psychologist, a special-education teacher, an administrator). If additional staff members will be attending the conference, tell parents before the meeting. This will help prevent parents from feeling overwhelmed and outnumbered.

Communicate with Parents and Students

Prepare for Substitute Teachers

Sooner or later, even the most devoted teacher spends a day away from the classroom for training, a planning day, illness, or personal business. Proper planning in advance will save you time later. When students are on task and on schedule while you are gone, they stay that way when you return. The following ideas and advice will help you prepare efficiently and effectively for a day when you need to be out of the classroom and have someone else attempt to fill your shoes.

Find a Trusted Substitute

Find an experienced substitute teacher you and your students like. Schedule him or her for the days you know you will be out as far in advance as you can so your students typically get the same substitute. Your students will appreciate the continuity, and you will be able to entrust this teacher with your "real" lesson plans. Have this teacher do the very same projects in the very same way you planned to. Since he or she knows your program more intimately than a one-time substitute would, he or she will be successful in a way that someone else could not be. With minimal disruption of their day, your students are more likely to carry on as they would with you than to view the day as "a day off."

Create a Substitute Teacher Folder

Every teacher needs a substitute teacher folder. You never know when you may be out unexpectedly. The following items should be included in this folder:

- class list

- map of the school with key areas marked (e.g., yard duty, staff lounge, teachers' workroom)

- disaster information (e.g., fire drill/earthquake procedures)

- seating chart and name tags

- school forms (e.g., office passes, lunch tickets)

- directions to the staff bathroom

Your folder should also include a simple lesson plan for an unexpected absence. Your plan should include activities that are easy enough for any teacher to follow, such as a class set of a math sheet and directions for conducting silent reading, journal writing, or creative writing with a list of topics. Leave detailed instructions on how you have students read (e.g., aloud as a class, volunteers, in pairs). Include a list of students the teacher may call upon for help locating materials or learning other class procedures. Instead of having this substitute tackle important content areas for which you may have special projects in mind, photocopy an article of interest to students about a topic you do not intend to teach. A high student-interest level will help the substitute teacher maintain on-task behavior with your students, and students will perceive the teacher as one who brings them fun and interesting work. This will reflect well on you.

Use a two-pocket folder to organize all of the items for the substitute folder. Laminate the permanent pages for durability. Place student worksheets in one pocket. Place the laminated information sheets and lesson plan in the other pocket. Be sure to write at the top of your lesson plan *Use these plans if no other plans have been provided.* In the event you are absent, your classroom will carry on almost as usual.

Keep Need-to-Know Information Handy

Record procedural information on index cards. Laminate the cards for durability, hole-punch them, and place them on a key ring. Hole-punch the corner of your substitute teacher folder, and secure the ring to the folder. Encourage the substitute teacher to remove the ring from the folder and flip through the cards for information as he or she has students get settled. Breaking the information up this way will help your substitute teacher quickly find and make use of the resources you have left him or her. Information to put on index cards includes

- class schedule. Make a different card for each day of the week. Be sure to highlight any duties you may have, such as yard or cafeteria duty.

- classroom rules.

- rewards and discipline plan.

- list of helpful teachers and their room and classroom phone numbers.

- schedule listing students who leave the classroom for special services or teachers who come into the classroom to provide those services and the times for each.

- schedule listing assistants or other people who come to work in the room and the times for each.

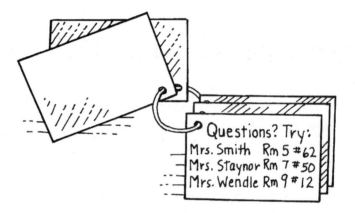

Make a Substitute Box

Write *Substitute Kit* and *Use anything in this box to help your day go smoothly* on a label. Place the label on a file box. Fill the box with a few good activities (and related materials) that are easy for someone unfamiliar with your class to do. Include a few good read-aloud books, a class set of fun paper activities (e.g., crossword puzzles, anagrams, geometric designs, coloring papers, math papers, a set of children's magazines or newspapers), and a simple art project (including all necessary art supplies). Add 8½" x 11" (21.5 cm x 28 cm) lined paper and 12" x 18" (30.5 cm x 46 cm) drawing paper to complete the box.

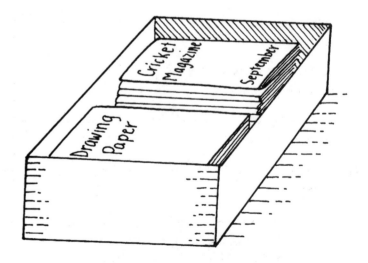

Happiness comes of the capacity to feel deeply, to enjoy simply, to think freely, to risk life, to be needed.
—Storm Jameson

You're Off!—The First Day

At last, the day has arrived, butterflies and all! With these terrific ideas and activities, your first day will fly by. Before you know it, you will have learned all those names, rules will be in place, learning will begin, and someone will tell you that you are his or her favorite teacher!

Go the Extra Mile for the First Day

The first day can be hectic. See the sample first-day schedule on page 40 for ideas on how you might schedule your day. Then, refer to the following tips to help it run smoothly:

■ Make a separate lesson plan just for the first day. List the schedule on a board or a chart so you can mark off events as a class. Keep it to look at for next year.

■ Do not go over *all* of the rules the first day. Have students help write rules they think will help their classroom work better, and introduce the procedural dos and don'ts before the first time they will be needed.

■ Have students write and agree on the class rules before the first recess.

■ Post a note on the door with the dismissal time for parents.

■ Leave a bulletin board blank for posting students' first work.

■ Have a funny, lighthearted book ready to read.

■ Let parents help organize the school supplies. Do not take up class time that could be better spent.

■ Allow small amounts of time throughout the day for students to share summer happenings, instead of all at once. They love to share, but they may not be too good at listening for long periods of time.

■ Take time to smile and let students know that you are excited about having them in your class. Share some of the fun activities planned for the year.

Find a little time each day to take a breather. For example, rest during recess instead of running around. You will be more productive in the long run. Know the big picture, but break it down into manageable bites.

Sample First-Day Schedule

8:45–9:00 Students enter—schoolhouse coloring pages on tables

9:00–9:15 Calendar

9:15–10:00 Class Meeting
- Introduce icebreaker activity
- Discuss expectations/Create class rules

10:00–10:20 Recess

10:20–10:40 Shared Reading
- Read aloud *Brown Bear, Brown Bear* by Bill Martin Jr.
- Play a color word game

10:40–11:20 Writing Workshop
- Teach mini-lesson—overview of writing workshop
- Write and conference quietly
- Introduce sharing

11:20–11:50 Lunch

11:50–12:10 Teacher Read-Aloud

12:10–1:00 Math
- Teach problem-solving activity
- Review numbers
  Read aloud *Anno's Counting Book* by Mitsumasa Anno

1:00–1:45 Reading Workshop
- Read aloud *First Day, Hooray!* by Nancy Poydar
- Introduce centers

1:45–2:15 P. E.

2:15–2:45 Working with words
- Read a rhyming book
- Review rhyming words with a circle game

2:45–3:00 Pack up to go home

3:00 Dismissal

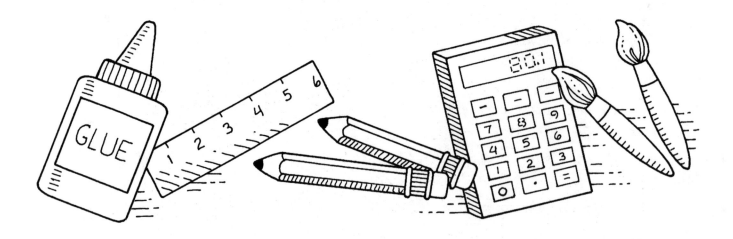

 Work with students on procedures before curriculum instruction. Research shows teachers who spend more time early in the year teaching classroom procedures and expectations make up the time later by losing far fewer minutes to problem behavior throughout the school year.

Keep Order

On the first day, assign each student a number to coordinate with the order in which he or she appears in your roll or record book. Here are some ways these numbers will come in handy:

- Whenever you collect papers call numbers instead of names. They will be in order, and you will have an easy tool for identifying missing papers.

- Teach students to write their name and their number on every paper. Have a file box with legal-size hanging file folders in an accessible spot. Provide a folder for each student with his or her number clearly marked. Initially, it will be easier for students to find their number. Have students file their corrected papers in their folder. On Friday, shortly before dismissal, stand by the file box, pull out each stack of papers, staple them together (or place them in a homework envelope, see page 28), and hand students their papers.

- Write a number inside books you distribute to students. Have each student take the book that matches his or her class number. Later, books separated from their owners can be easily returned to the students who lost them.

- Use the numbers to combine lining up with number play. For example, invite the student whose number is the answer to your question (e.g., 2+5, the numbers in today's date, all the even numbers, all the odd numbers) to line up. This is also a fast and fun way to teach more advanced students the concept of multiples.

 As soon as possible, put your class list into your emergency backpack (page 10). Be prepared for an emergency from the first to the last day of school.

Invite First-Day Help

Parents are full of mixed emotions when they leave their student at school on the first day. Place a *Help Needed* sign on the door so parents cannot miss seeing it. Have ready a list of jobs that need to be done. This provides a great opportunity for volunteers to feel they are part of a team effort from day one, and they are able to get to know how much you appreciate their help! Wrap a cookie, biscotti, or muffin with a tea bag and ribbon, and attach a note of thanks. You have gotten things off to a great start, and you will not have to stay unnecessarily late in your classroom.

Be Prepared for a Change in Grade Levels

Sometimes your straight first grade becomes a first/second combination class after one or two weeks of school. Develop a theme for the beginning of the year, such as Fairy Tales, that you can easily adapt to several grade levels. This will help you organize your curriculum and schedule.

Teach the Class to Find You

Teach the class a special whistle signal that means "Look for Your Teacher!" This becomes helpful when many classes are on the playground at one time. A familiar whistle signal (e.g., two short blows on the whistle) alerts your class that you are trying to get their attention.

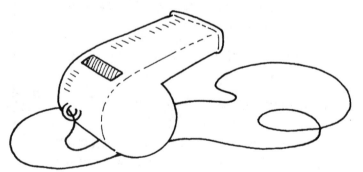

Place a clipboard with paper by the door. Sometimes five or six parents will want to tell you about allergies, student custody issues, and day-care arrangements all at once. Ask them to write down important information. You can check messages once the class is on task.

Manage School Supplies

If you have students bring in school supplies at the start of the year, use the School Supply Checklist reproducible (page 97) to keep track of students' school supplies as they come in. Have students use tape or a permanent marker to label their supplies and place the supplies in a designated area until you check them in. After two weeks, write a short, generic reminder to parents and leave a blank space to fill in the specific supplies missing for each student. Photocopy the reminder, and use the checklist to quickly and efficiently make a personalized note.

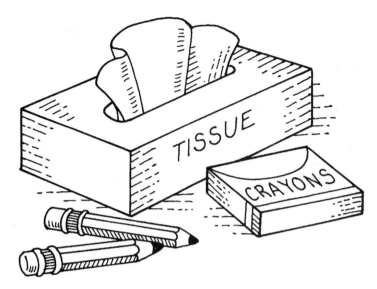

Take First-Day Photos

Take a separate photo of each student on the first day of school. Use your photos for the following ideas:

- When students return to school on the second day, display the photos with a catchy title such as

  - *Look Who's New in Room 2!*

  - *Our New Crop!* (Place each student's picture in an apple.)

  - *Room 6 Starring . . .* (Place each student's picture in a star.)

- Type each student's name on his or her photo, and laminate it for durability. Use the photos to graph attendance, hair color, eye color, favorites (e.g., types of bugs, music, places to vacation), and more.

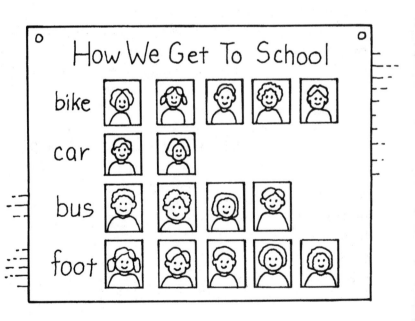

 Photocopy each student's emergency card before you turn it in to the office. The information on the card is important for you to have handy in your own files.

Bulletin Boards and Wall Displays

Bulletin boards and wall displays set the tone for the classroom. They celebrate work done, skills learned, and the people in the classroom. Be sure you clearly label everything you display so visitors can see at a glance the curriculum, skills, and volume of work represented. This section contains bulletin boards and other static or interactive displays specially designed for the first days of school, as well as how-tos for displaying student work all year long.

I Am Special!

Give each student a photocopy of the I Am Special reproducible (page 98). Invite students to decorate the figure on the sheet with art supplies (e.g., wallpaper or drapery samples, scraps of fabric, glue, wiggly eyes, paint, crayons or markers, buttons) and cut it out. Give students tagboard clothing patterns to help them make clothing for their self-portrait. Distribute one 6" x 3" (15 cm x 7.5 cm) brown and one 5" x 2" (12.5 cm x 5 cm) black rectangle of construction paper to each student. Invite students to write their name with a white crayon or chalk on the black rectangle and then glue the black paper on top of the brown one, leaving a small part of brown showing around the black. Give each student a sticker to add to his or her "chalkboard" name tag. Have students put a dot of glue on each hand of the paper doll and place the chalkboard on the glue. For added fun, take the dolls down before Back-to-School Night and attach them to the front of a folder for each student's family.

 # Frame Me!

Give each student a photocopy of the Frame Me reproducible (page 99). Provide a variety of art supplies, and have students create a self-portrait on the first day of school. For added fun, invite them to use stickers or rubber stamps to add a seasonal touch. Have students write or dictate about how they have grown over the summer. Then, display students' self-portraits and writing on a bulletin board. Repeat the activity at the end of every month. Save the self-portraits and writing after you take them down, and have a parent help you compile each student's work into a book. Display the books at Open House. Invite students and parents to enjoy the growth they see in the detail of the drawings.

Can-Do Kids

Encourage students to have a "can-do" attitude by creating a personalized bulletin board that spotlights their strengths. Give each student a photocopy of the Can Do reproducible (page 100). Have students write their name and something they do well on the reproducible. Give students a piece of drawing paper, and ask them to draw a picture to go with their writing. Cover a large can with light-colored butcher paper. Label the can *These Kids Can Do Anything!* Cover the bulletin board area with bright-colored paper, and then add a contrasting border. Use large thumbtacks to attach the can to the middle of the board, and arrange students' papers around it.

Thematic Border

Invite students to help you create a custom-made bulletin board border. Have students use paint and sponges (or potatoes cut into thematic shapes), stamps, stickers, and crayons or markers to create designs on white or colored adding machine tape or narrow strips of butcher paper. Laminate the finished border for durability.

The Alphabet around Us

Take pictures of places in your town or community that begin with each letter of the alphabet. Add these pictures to a bulletin board, or use them to initiate daily interactive writing as follows: Attach each photo to a large piece of construction paper along with a large letter of the alphabet, and laminate. Each day, pull out a new letter, discuss the place, and have students brainstorm a sentence about that place. Write the sentence on adding machine tape. Tape the sentence to the paper under the picture. Every day, before writing about the new location, reread the previous sentences. This helps students develop writing skills, awareness of high-frequency words, and concepts about print.

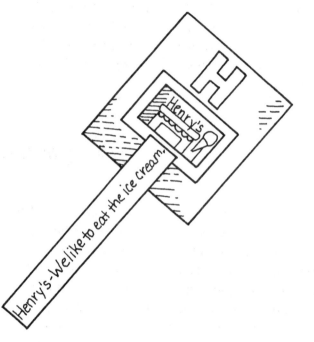

Assemble a Photo Alphabet

On the first day of school, take a close-up photo of each student and include yourself and any class pets. Make and display an alphabet frieze of capital letters. Have students read the room, saying the letters and the names. For example, *A—Adam, Ashley, B—Brian, Brett, Brianna.* Display all letters even if you do not have a name for each letter.

The Living Alphabet

During the first week of school, invite the class to look around the room for things and people that start with each letter of the alphabet. Take a picture of each one, and use these photos in a bulletin board display titled *The Living Alphabet*. Glue a second set of the pictures on the inside and outside of a file folder, and laminate the folder. Then, send it home for parents to look at. For extra fun, do this with the pictures you take of students doing various classroom activities. This gives parents who cannot get into the classroom an opportunity to see what it is like.

Friendship Train

Give each student a photocopy of the Train Car reproducible (page 101), and have students cut out the train car. Invite them to decorate their train cars with art supplies (e.g., wallpaper or drapery samples, scraps of fabric, glue, paint, crayons or markers, buttons). Next, photograph each student or encourage students to paint a self-portrait. Title the bulletin board *Friendship Train*. Then, staple the train cars together on the bulletin board so they are all connected. Add the student pictures in or on each car. Now you are ready to add some writing. Invite students to write about any of the following topics: how they are a friend, what makes a friend, or *I like friends who are _____.* Display the writing with the trains. Photocopy the Train Engine reproducible (page 102) on bright paper, have a student decorate it, and add it to the front of the train. Save the trains for future bulletin boards with titles such as *Right on Track* or *Working Together.*

Starring Our Class!

Cover a bulletin board with butcher paper. Cut 3" x 12" (7.5 cm x 30.5 cm) strips of yellow construction paper. These will become the border. Have each student sign his or her name on a strip with different-colored markers. Staple the strips around the bulletin board to form a border. Add some glitter-glue stars if possible. Give students star templates, and have each student trace a star from his or her favorite color of construction paper and cut it out. Provide pattern scissors for extra fun. Invite students to draw a picture of themselves in the middle of their star. In each corner, have them write one word that tells something about them. Display the stars on the bulletin board under a title such as *Starring Our Class.* To get a 3-D effect, attach small paper cups behind some of the stars and then attach them to the butcher paper.

Everyone's a Star!

Have students brainstorm things they do well or enjoy. List their responses on the chalkboard. Give each student a copy of the Star reproducible (page 103). Have students draw themselves doing an activity and complete the sentence frame about the activity. Have them write their own name in the first blank of the sentence frame. Display the papers on a board titled *Everyone's a Star!* Later, when you take the bulletin board display down, place the pictures in a class book.

Fall into a Good Book

Try this display idea on a wall near your reading corner:

1. Create a 3-D tree out of wire, brown butcher paper, and green butcher paper. Place it against a bulletin board. Staple fishing line around the tree and into the wall to make the tree stable. Alternatively, sponge-paint a tree on construction paper, or use a premade tree.

2. Cut out assorted colors of construction or butcher paper leaves, or wait until the first day of school and invite students to sponge-paint fall leaves to be added to the board.

3. Write titles of books the class reads on the leaves, or display the book covers or books on the bulletin board along with the scattered leaves. If you make the board prior to the first day of school, attach the books you plan to read with T-pins (one on the top and bottom) and hang real fall leaves.

4. As you read the books or add books, invite students to write book reviews to add to the board.

5. If you plan on changing this board with each season, show the changing seasons on the tree.

6. Make a growing border out of the title of each read-aloud book using small construction paper rectangles to resemble books.

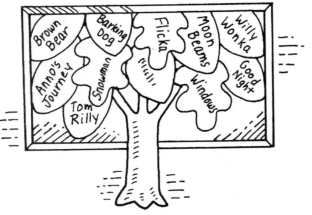

Solve the Problem of Hard Walls

Some classrooms have hard walls that resist staples and tacks (e.g., cinderblock walls). Here are several solutions that do not involve power equipment or staple guns:

- Purchase a roll of cork at a home improvement store. Nail or hot-glue the cork to the wall.

- Nail 1/4" (6 mm) sheets of plywood to the wall, and cover the plywood with butcher paper or fabric.

- Use tacky gum adhesive to hang laminated posters and artwork.

- Use adhesive-backed Velcro for pocket charts and posters. Place one side of the Velcro on the wall and the other side on the item you will display.

- Brush rubber cement on the back of butcher paper or laminated materials. When you take the piece down, the rubber cement will rub off easily.

Make Word Walls

Learning to read "the writing on the wall" is an effective way to expose students to a wide variety of new and frequently used words. Word walls are an inventive and dynamic way to immerse students in language. Creating a word wall involves students adding a few words each week to a wall or bulletin board. Old words remain as new words are added. The result is a learning tool that is constantly being constructed and reconstructed through-out the year. Here are a few ideas for creating a word wall for your room:

Organize words
- alphabetically

- by word families

- by parts of speech (e.g., nouns, adjectives, adverbs, verbs)

- by commonly used words

- by commonly misspelled words or homophones

- by theme

Words for the word wall can be
- computer generated

- written on sentence strips or index cards

To attach words to the wall, use
- pushpins

- double-sided tape

- tacky gum adhesive

- adhesive-backed Velcro

Arrange word walls
- in straight lines on the wall.

- against the backdrop of a large thematic drawing.

- on a moveable wall. (Cover a large piece of plywood with fabric or carpeting, and put adhesive-backed Velcro on the back of your word cards.)

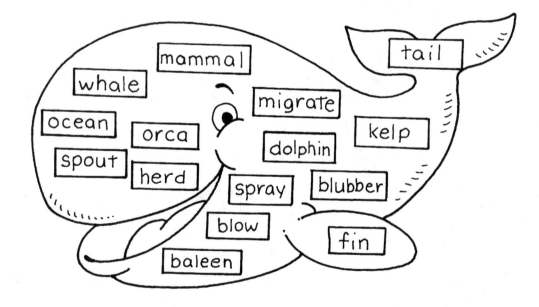

Break the Ice

The following activities serve two purposes: They help you learn your students' names and personalities, and they help the class come together as a group. Read each activity, and choose the ones that appeal to you. Then, schedule them often during the first weeks of school.

Apple Mixer

Photocopy the Apples reproducible (page 104) on various colors of construction paper. Make at least four apples of each color and enough altogether for one for each student. Hole-punch one hole in four apples, two holes in four apples, three holes in four apples, and so on until all the apples have holes. Next, place matching stickers on sets of four apples, varying apple color and number of holes until each apple has a unique combination of color, number of holes, and stickers. Invite each student to choose an apple. Then, ask students to find someone with the same color apple and find out their partner's name. Have them introduce each other to the class. Next, ask students to find a person whose apple has the same number of holes as their own and find out what their partner's favorite food is. Encourage students to share what they learned with the class. Finally, ask students to find a student whose apple has the same type of sticker and ask their partner's favorite color. Invite sharing again. At the end of the activity, use double-stick tape to turn the apples into name tags.

51

Welcome Students with Open Arms

Communicate to students from the very beginning that they are important to you. Find clip art that suits your personality and will make students smile. Photocopy the clip art onto an overhead transparency, and project it on a large sheet of tagboard. Color in the clip art. Come up with a creative heading, such as *Mrs.* *Smith's Sweeties* or *Mr. Drew's Crew.* Laminate your welcome chart before you write students' names on it and you will be able to use it year after year. Write students' names with an erasable marker. Be there with hugs or high fives to greet the kids when they find their name on your list.

A Tough Egg to Crack

Have students sit in a circle, and explain to them the term icebreaker. Tell students that today they will break eggs, instead, to help them get to know each other. Fill a plastic egg for each student with a piece of paper with a question about a classmate, you, another faculty member, or the school (e.g., *What is the name of our principal? Which student or students in our class have a first name that starts with the letter A? What object appears in each classroom in our school?).* Have students take turns "cracking" their egg, reading their question aloud, and answering the question. Encourage students to ask their classmates for help if necessary.

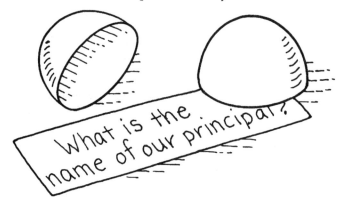

True or False

Have students write one false and two true sentences about themselves and take turns reading them to the class. Invite the class to guess which statement is false. This can also be conducted as a small-group activity. Invite students to write two false and five true sentences about their group and read their sentences to the class. Encourage the class to try to identify the false statements. Or, have individuals in the group tell their sentences to each other and encourage other group members to identify the true and false sentences.

Just like Me

Give each student a copy of the Just like Me reproducible (page 105). Have students fill in the blanks in the *Me* column. Then, have students find classmates who have the same answers and write the name of the student with the matching answer in the appropriate blank in the *Just like Me* column.

Me	Just like Me
Eye Color brown	Steve
Hair Color black	Jun
Favorite Sport soccer	Hadley
Favorite Season summer	Mrs. Williams

Friendship Necklaces

Obtain four large bags of ziti pasta, and spray-paint the ziti from two bags gold and the remaining ziti silver. Cut 3' (1 m) pieces of string, and tape the ends. Cut 4" (10 cm) diameter circles from construction paper or card stock, and tie string to one end of each circle. Have students string silver and gold ziti to make pattern necklaces. While students make their necklaces, have them sing or chant this song:

Make new friends, but keep the old.
One is silver and the other's gold.
A circle is round. It has no end.
That's how long I want to be your friend.
Forever and ever!

Tie the free end of the string to the other side of the paper circle. Make several copies of the Friends reproducible (page 106), and cut out a circle for each student. Then, have students fill in their circle with a new friend's name and complete the sentence frame. Have students glue their circle to their necklace to complete the project. Invite students to wear their necklace home on their first day.

Today I made a
new friend named
_____.

We like to
_____.

Getting to Know You

On the first day of school, plan to have students sit in a circle on the floor and tell each other a few things about themselves. Put treats into a bag or basket. Have students pass the bag or basket around the circle. Invite each student to choose up to five of the treats. For each treat students choose, ask them to say one thing about themselves. Go first to model your expectations. For example, choosing five treats, you might say

I have a dog and a guinea pig at my house.
I love to read and write.
My favorite color is blue.
My favorite food is pepperoni pizza.
I am so excited to see all of my new friends!

I Spy Fun

Invite students to tape two small cardboard tubes to make their own "binoculars." Have each student hole-punch each side of two tubes. Give students yarn, and have them tie each end to a hole. Hang a pair of binoculars around your neck, and invite students to join you at a writing chart. Have students use their binoculars to spy something they think would be fun to do at school. Add each student's ideas to a list on the chart. Include activities that would take place both inside and outside the classroom. Excitement builds with this activity as students think together about the fun they will have at school! Challenge students to add more to the class list later in the day as they think of more fun activities.

Silly Name Sentences

Pick a name from the class list each day. Write a student's name on the top of a chart. Circle the first letter of the name. Have the class brainstorm words that begin with that letter, and list them on the chart. Then, challenge students to create a silly sentence with as many of the words as possible (e.g., *Gaby made me eat green grasshopper gum and I got grumpy!*). Write the sentence on a large sheet of construction paper, and have the student illustrate his or her silly sentence.

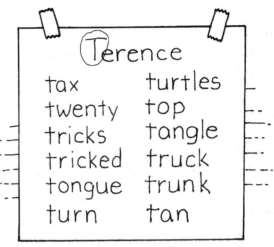

(T)erence
tax	turtles
twenty	top
tricks	tangle
tricked	truck
tongue	trunk
turn	tan

Terence tricked twenty-two turtles into turning.

Name Bingo

Write on a photocopy of the Names reproducible (page 107) names of students, faculty, and places in the school. Photocopy a class set of this master. Distribute a photocopy of the Bingo reproducible (page 108) and a revised Names sheet to each student. Ask students to cut out the names and choose 24 to glue to the squares on the board to make a completed bingo card. Cut apart your Names sheet, shuffle the names, and place them facedown on your desk. Give each student pennies, beans, or other small items to use as markers. Draw a name, call it out, and have students find and cover the name on their card. After someone wins a game by covering five names in a straight line in any direction, have students swap their card with a classmate and play again. Small candies, raffle tickets, new pencils, and "lunch with the teacher" coupons make fun prizes for this game.

Name _____

B	I	N	G	O
Paul	Mr. Cook	Alicia	Ryan	Carly
Aubrey	Marc	◯	Lupe	Jack
Mrs. Stuart	Maria	☼	Mario	Rhian
Lydia	Raul	◯	Alex	Lacey
Jesus	Rose	Jill	John	Mrs. King

Establish Procedures and Routines

Every teacher has a unique way of doing things. Students arrive wanting to know how things are done in your room. If you tell them clearly and follow up those expectations consistently, before you know it, your students will be responsibly and respectfully running at least some of the classroom all by themselves. Your plants will be watered, your books will be straightened, your students will quiet down when you give directions. Use the tried-and-true ideas in this section to make your classroom run smoothly.

Teach Transitions

An effective transition signal that quiets students so they can hear the next set of directions you give does not involve raising your voice. A raised voice encourages more raised voices. Try these simple tips to get students' attention in a positive way:

- Use a rain stick to get students' attention. Tell students that when they hear the rain stick, they should put their hands together and then be still.

- Use a windup music box to get your students' attention. Every Monday, wind up the music box. When you need the class to be quiet, open the music box. As soon as they have quieted down, close the box. Explain that if there is music left in the box by the end of the week, the class will earn a reward.

- Play music as students come in from recess. Reward the class with a point if all students are seated, quiet, and attentive at the end of the song. As students respond more quickly to the signal, you can use shorter pieces of music.

- Play each note on a xylophone to signal students to listen for further directions.

- Use rhymes to have students transition from one activity to another. Say the first part of a rhyme (they will quickly quiet to hear which one you will say), and invite them to finish it. For example, you say *Little Bo Peep* and students reply *lost her sheep,* and then they move to the next activity.

- For older students, write one letter of a word at a time and teach them to be seated by the end of the word. If your class has a team name, that works well. For example, if your class is named Sea Stars, write on the board S-e-a-S-t-a-r-s. All should be at attention by the last *s*.

 Identify a spot on the floor where you will stand only when you want students' attention. Stand there, hold up your hand, and silently count to five on your fingers, by which time they should be attentive. Post a chart with guidelines such as *1—pencils down, 2—mouths closed, 3—chairs turned toward teacher, 4—hands in lap, 5—listening.*

- Teach students to copy your clapping or snapping pattern. The tactile signal helps them focus.

 # Get Students Home

Schools differ in how they get students home. Check first with your school office regarding official rules and routines. In the absence of an existing structure, here are two ideas for getting your students safely home:

■ Most schools have several ways students go home: in a car, on a bike, in a bus, in a day care van, on foot, on skates, or even on skateboards. Teachers need to know where each student goes on each day and how he or she gets there. Have parents complete a Transportation reproducible (page 109), and then make a list or bulletin board display with the five days of the week and how each student leaves school. Divide the class into three groups: *With Parent, Bus or Van,* and *Self-propelled.* Being organized will get your students safely home.

■ If most of your students are picked up by car, here is a system your whole school can implement. Make a sign for each student on colored card stock with each teacher's initial written with a large dark marker on the top half. Write the student's first name on the bottom half with the same marker. Have the appropriate drivers place the card in the front window of their cars. Post a teacher at the entrance to the pick-up area, and have him or her call out the name on the arriving car. Have a second teacher escort the appropriate student to the curb. Have the driver drive to the waiting student. Have the teacher open the door for the student and wish him or her a good day. Traffic keeps moving and students are safe.

 If your classroom is not equipped with hooks or hangers, minimize lost jackets and backpacks by labeling five baskets with numbers and placing them outside the classroom. Assign each student a basket to place his or her belongings in. Bring the baskets in when students arrive, and stack them in a corner.

Establish Procedures and Routines

Keep Track of Lunch Plans

Decide where to locate your lunch graph, and give students easy access to it. Use ¼" (6 mm) detail tape to apply a grid to the front of your desk or the side of a tall file cabinet. Make sure the grid is large enough to accommodate a magnet for each student, and leave space at the top. Write *What's for Lunch?* above the grid using adhesive letters or double-sided tape and laminated letters. Provide each student with a small boy or girl cutout from the Lunchtime reproducible (page 110) to color. Laminate the paper dolls, and attach a magnetic strip to the back of each one. Color and cut out the lunch box and bag, home, and lunch tray from the reproducible, laminate the cutouts, and attach a magnetic strip to each one. Have students place their character on the chart next to the icon that represents their lunch choice (i.e., bringing from home, purchasing lunch, going home for lunch) every morning for a graph of your lunch count.

Prepare No Homework Cards

Photocopy on card stock a stack of the No Homework Card reproducible (page 111). Cut the cards in half to make individual No Homework Cards, and place the cards in a file folder or envelope for storage. Throughout the year when you have reason to cancel homework, stamp the No Homework Cards with the date and send them home with students. Be sure to show parents the card when you discuss your homework policy at Back-to-School Night. Parents can be sure that, unless they see that card, there is homework to be done.

Create Classroom Jobs

Classrooms operate much like families. Each individual has certain rights and responsibilities within the classroom unit. The responsibilities involve working together to perform the daily tasks necessary to help the unit function efficiently and effectively. Classroom jobs are a means of naming, delegating, and managing these tasks. When students complete classroom jobs, they develop a sense of active participation in the classroom family. You are also relieved of the added duty of managing daily chores. Many chores need to be done each day. Some jobs will only need to be completed once or twice a week. The first step in determining what jobs you will need is to brainstorm a list of all the tasks performed regularly. Such a list might include the following:

- taking attendance

- leading lines

- straightening the classroom library

- returning library books

- watering classroom plants

- feeding class pets

- carrying playground equipment to recess

- filing completed and corrected work

Write your job list on an overhead transparency. Ask students to review the list and add any additional suggestions. Once your job list is complete, copy it onto a large poster and laminate it. Hang the chart in a prominent place in the classroom. Write students' names on the poster with a washable marker.

 Give your students responsibility and they will feel more ownership of the classroom. They will live up to your expectations, so keep them high.

Assign and Rotate Classroom Jobs

Students will be anxious to jump in and get to work. Now comes the task of establishing a routine for assigning and rotating the jobs. Make sure the method you select is manageable for the entire year. Here are a few suggestions for job assignments:

■ Place two large jars on your desk. Label one *Job Jar #1* and the other *Job Jar #2*. Write each student's name on a small card. Place all the cards in Jar #1. Draw student names from the jar to fill each job. When a name is drawn, place it into Jar #2. Each week, select a new group of students to fill the jobs. When the first jar is empty, reverse the process by drawing names from Jar #2. This way, students will be assigned jobs an equal number of times.

■ Place slips of paper with all student names in a hat. Select a name, and give the student ten seconds to select a job. Repeat this process until all jobs are filled. Do not replace the names of students who have been selected. Draw new names each week until all students have held a job. Begin again by filling the hat with all students' names.

■ Create a giant construction paper or butcher paper ladder, and attach it to the wall. Label each rung of the ladder with a classroom job. Write each student's name on a footprint cutout. Place the cutouts in a large envelope at the bottom of the ladder, and place another large envelope at the top of the ladder. Begin by choosing cutouts for each job. Tape the footprints on the rung for the corresponding job. Each week, move students up the ladder one rung and select a new footprint from the envelope at the bottom of the ladder to fill the first job. Place the footprint from the top rung into the envelope at the top of the ladder. When the bottom envelope is empty, exchange it with the envelope at the top.

■ Use the cardboard circle from a take-out pizza box to prepare a tool for keeping track of classroom jobs. Divide the circle into the number of sections that reflect the number of students in the class. (Consider adding a few extra spaces for late additions to the roster.) Write each job on a space on the circle. (If there are not enough jobs for each section, scatter the jobs around the circle.) Attach a piece of Velcro to the end of each section. Write each student's name on a small piece of cardboard, attach a piece of Velcro to the back of the cardboard, and place each on a section in the circle. Each week, rotate the names around the circle to give each student a new job. (Some students may not have a job each week.)

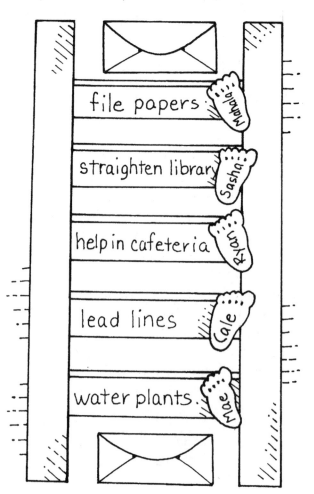

Create Student Groups

Cooperative grouping is an effective way for students to learn how to work together to achieve a common goal. Collaboration or "group work" provides a vehicle for students to problem-solve, improve oral communication, and learn to be an integral group member. Classroom groupings also promote positive peer relationships that create a nurturing environment for learning while diminishing common classroom problems. Students can and should be in more than one group at a time. Here are some grouping options:

- A family group is made up of four or five students who remain together for the entire school year. They meet daily to write in their journals, fill out assignment notebooks, collect homework for absent group members, and problem-solve classroom issues. This group provides a constant base for students and helps form positive, lasting peer relationships.

- A home group is a long-term group of four or five students who stay together for at least two weeks and at most the length of a grading period. Invite students to choose the members of this group, assign them to groups, or use a system such as a sociogram. (Have students write a confidential list of five students they would like to have in their group and one student they choose not to sit with. Promise them one of the students in the first group and that they will not sit with the student they chose not to sit with. No class is unanimous in their dislike of one student. With careful planning, you will be able to meet this promise. After two weeks, rearrange groups that are not earning a reasonable number of points for responsible, on-task behavior.)

- An academic group is a temporary group established to meet a short-term goal. This group comes together to work on a specific skill and then disbands.

- An interest group is formed when students share a common interest and come together for further study. This group is especially useful for establishing curriculum-based project groups. For example, students studying communities may group themselves according to interest. Some students may wish to learn more about community government, some may wish to learn about firefighters and police, and others may select to study families. Groups work on their interest area and then share their research with the whole class.

- A service group is a small number of students selected to work together to complete a specific classroom task. A group may come together to organize the classroom library. Another group may be assigned the job of cleaning the class pets' cages. These are temporary groups that are usually assigned one task.

Students may be grouped by ability in either homogeneous or heterogeneous groups. Remember that a variety of grouping options provides students with the best overall learning experience. Always provide ways for students to assess their group's progress. Have students assess the work they accomplished and the ability of their group to work as a team.

Establish Procedures and Routines

Plan Field Trips

Field trips are special days. They require careful planning, as early as possible. A well-planned field trip will encourage more parents to volunteer for the next one and you'll have fun, too. Try these teacher-tested ideas for field-trip success:

■ Have students dress alike for a field trip. At least have students all wear the same color pants and shirts (e.g., blue jeans and white shirts). For a terrific beginning-of-the-year class-unity project, have each student bring in a white T-shirt. Die all the shirts bright yellow—the die is inexpensive and directions are on the box—and have students use sponge paint to decorate the shirts with themes that reflect your expected field trips (e.g., animals for the trip to the zoo, a baseball bat for the trip to the game at the end of the year). Encourage students to bring in a shirt that is a little big for them so they do not grow out of it by the end of the year. Wash the shirts yourself after each trip or have a parent volunteer do it. If you send them home, these beloved shirts may not come back.

■ Find out what field trips other teachers in your grade level are taking and what trips teachers in the grade levels before you have taken. Avoid taking students places they went last year, and coordinate with teachers in your own grade level to travel together. Sharing buses and the responsibility for phone calls or fund-raising can be a big help. If you are a new teacher, find out what field trips the previous teacher took (and what units they were tied to) and decide whether you want to continue these traditions.

■ Divide the class into small groups with a parent chaperone assigned to each group. Give each adult a list of the children he or she is responsible for, and give each driver a map with written directions. Do not assign yourself a group. Your job is to oversee the class and the adults.

■ If you are taking a bus to your destination, bring a box with trash bags and baby wipes. Have it on board in case of motion sickness.

■ Plan only a short time for lunch. Children eat quickly, and most field-trip destinations are not properly equipped for recess. Twenty minutes is probably enough.

■ Always take a first aid kit on field trips. Use a fanny pack to hold the medical supplies. If you are on a field trip where your groups will be separated, create a kit for each chaperone.

 Do not schedule field trips for Mondays or Fridays. These are transition days. Weekends can be stressful for kids, even if it is "good" stress. On Mondays students need a day to get back into the school frame of mind, and on Fridays they are already anticipating the weekend.

Manage Bathroom Breaks and Getting Drinks

Requests to go to the bathroom or get drinks may interrupt lessons and learning. However, you need to know where your students are at all times, and you need to know if students are abusing this privilege. These tried-and-true systems encourage students to get drinks and use the bathroom as they need to and allow you to monitor students without disrupting learning:

■ Write each student's name on a craft stick. Divide the name sticks into two containers, one labeled *boys* and one labeled *girls*. Decorate three other containers. (Cans or plastic cups work well.) Label one container *Boy's Bathroom*, label the second *Girl's Bathroom*, and label the third *Drinks*. When students need to use the restroom or get a drink, they move their stick into the appropriate container. If someone's stick is already in the container, students should wait for that person to return to the room.

■ Write each student's name on a clothespin. Attach a piece of rope to the wall next to the door. Have the rope hang down so all students can reach it. Attach the clothespins to the rope. Create cardboard icons to represent the boy's bathroom, the girl's bathroom, and the drinking fountain. Hang these icons on or near the classroom door. When students need to use the restroom or get a drink, they take their clothespin from the rope and clip it to the appropriate icon. If students break the rules or have behavior problems using this privilege, clip their clothespin to your shirt or pants. The students will then have to ask for their clothespin before using the bathroom or getting a drink. You will be able to closely monitor their coming and going.

■ Make two large cardboard keys. Label one key *Boys* and one key *Girls*. You may also wish to color-code the keys blue and pink. Hang the keys on hooks near the classroom door. When a student needs to use the restroom, he or she takes the appropriate key. Upon returning to the classroom, the student replaces the key on the hook.

■ Research shows that drinking water helps students maximize brain power. Invite students to keep a filled water bottle on their desk so they can have a drink whenever they need one. Generate with your students a list of rules for water bottles (e.g., water only, they may only fill it during their recess, lunch, or free time).

Set up Sharing

Assign students specific days for sharing or Show and Tell. Use students' self-portraits or photos or other visual aids to display the group of students sharing for each day. Place the groups on five different background colors (one for each day), and include the sharing day with each grouping. Send a note home to parents informing them of their child's sharing day and expectations regarding sharing.

Keep Student Participation Equal

Trim a small photo of each student into a circle, and attach each photo to one end of a colored tongue depressor or craft stick. Write the student's name on the stick with a permanent marker. Place students' name sticks in a cute container, photos up. During the course of the day, draw a stick to call on a student. Turn the stick photo down when the student has had a turn. Students will have equal opportunities to participate.

Write on index cards days and times each student has appointments for special services (e.g., a resource specialist program, a speech lesson, a counseling appointment, a music lesson). Stamp a clock face on the card with hands pointing to the correct time. Attach the card to the student's desk, and encourage each student to use the card as a reminder to be on time for appointments.

Begin a Take-Home Reading Program

To provide a way for parents and students to borrow books from your classroom library on a regular basis, write up a parent contract or use the Coaches' Contract (page 112) to motivate parents to participate and inform them of their responsibilities. Have parents and students sign and return this contract. Then, write each student's name on a resealable plastic bag. Place in the bag directions for any accompanying writing assignments, a photocopy of the Book Log reproducible (page 113), and two or three books at an appropriate reading level for that student (or invite students to choose their own books). Have an in-basket specifically for collecting the book bags each morning, and set aside a time each afternoon to distribute the bags. If sending home a new book every afternoon is too much, try sending home three or four books to be read and reread once a week.

65

Foster On-Target Behavior

Your classroom management system should make maintaining self-control, staying on-task, and being responsible look more attractive than any other option available. Because teachers have diverse styles of classroom management, ideas in this section offer different plans for maintaining a learning atmosphere. When setting up an incentive system, include rewards for

- individual achievement: a reward for an individual student who exceeds expectations (e.g., stickers, stamps, or points added to a card).

- small-group achievement: a reward shared among the members of a small group that meets or exceeds expectations (e.g., dropping marbles in a jar to earn a trip to the prize box).

- whole-class achievement: a reward shared by the class for behavior above and beyond expectations, or for consistently meeting a goal over a period of time (e.g., points added to a chart to earn a class movie).

Both the small-group and whole-class achievement rewards promote positive peer pressure and camaraderie. Post an easy-to-read description of the system, and inform those who visit and are involved with your students of your policies.

Discuss and Define Class Rules

Make your classroom rules meaningful and memorable to your class by involving students in the process of generating the rules. During the first days of the school year, brainstorm with students their classroom rights and responsibilities. Based on these rights and responsibilities, discuss acceptable and unacceptable classroom behavior. Then, generate together a set of class rules, keeping the following in mind:

- Keep rules brief.

- Generate broad rules.

- Keep rules few in number.

- Use a positive tone (i.e., tell what to do, rather than what not to do).

Test the usefulness of the rules and establish clear definitions of them by suggesting hypothetical situations in which students demonstrate acceptable and unacceptable behavior, and discuss as a class the rule to which each situation applies. Reword the rules as necessary to make sure all situations are addressed. Finally, number the rules and post them within all students' view. When students are in violation of a rule, simply hold up the number of fingers corresponding to the rule to avoid interrupting your lesson or train of thought. Because students were active in creating the rules, they will be much more likely to abide by them. The following is an example of an effective set of rules:

Rule 1: Be responsible.
Rule 2: Be respectful.
Rule 3: Be resourceful.
Rule 4: Be a risk-taker.

Pull Cards from Pockets

In an out-of-the-way corner of your classroom, create a small display with a library-card pocket labeled with each student's name. Place a stack of different-colored construction paper rectangles or index cards in each student's library-card pocket. (Make sure each stack has the same set of colors in the same order.) Add to the display a chart that coordinates each color with a behavioral consequence. For example:

■ Green: acceptable behavior

■ Yellow: warning (one rule violation)

■ Blue: ten-minute time out (two rule violations)

■ Orange: loss of recess (three rule violations)

■ Pink: stay ten minutes after school (four rule violations)

■ Red: removal from the classroom and a notice home (five rule violations)

Students start each morning with their first card showing. If they choose to violate a rule, nonchalantly ask them to "pull a card." This means that they silently walk to the display, place their first card at the back of their stack, and leave their second card showing. Each time they choose to violate a rule, they repeat this procedure and accept the consequences. This behavior-management program sets consistent, non-negotiable consequences; provides a visual reminder to students of their behavioral status; and allows you to mete out consequences without interrupting your task at hand or drawing attention to the inappropriate behavior. At the end of each day, record in a grade book each student's color, and reset the card stacks so the "acceptable behavior" card is at the front of each one. Consider rewarding students who maintain acceptable behavior for an entire week.

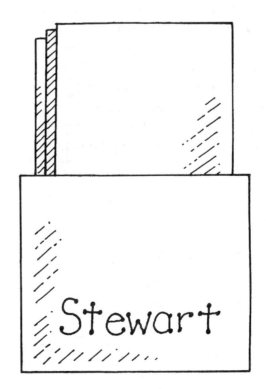

Build a Rainbow

In contrast to Pull Cards from Pockets on page 67, this behavior-management system focuses on positive reinforcement. For each student, make an arc of the rainbow in red, orange, yellow, green, blue, and purple construction paper. Make the red arc biggest and the purple smallest so that each color is ¹/₂" (13 mm) smaller than the previous color. Laminate the arcs if possible. Type each student's name on white paper, cut it out, and tape it on the inside of the plastic of a pocket chart. Place all of the rainbow pieces in a bucket or rainbow bag. When a student sets a good example (e.g., does an act of kindness, takes a learning risk), tell him or her to *Build a rainbow.* Have the student go to the bucket or bag, take out the next color, and place it in front of the previous color to add to his or her rainbow. (You may want to have a completed rainbow on display for students to use as a guide when adding the next appropriate color.) If a student breaks a class rule, have him or her take a color band away. When a student reaches purple, have the class cheer and clap for him or her. Send an award home with the student to notify parents that their child built a rainbow.

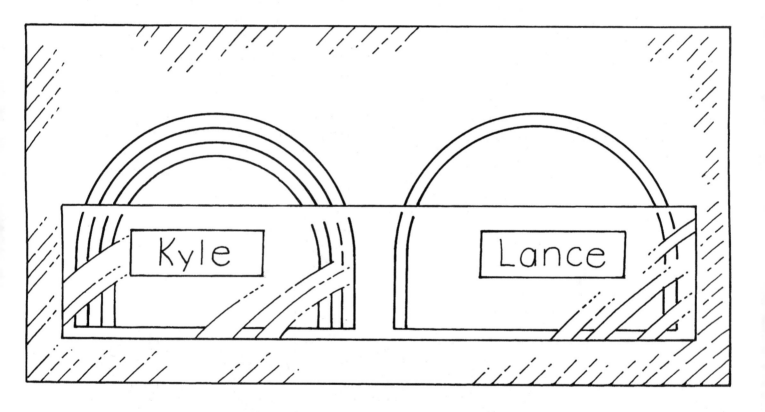

 Using a nonverbal signal will often diffuse a power struggle, does not disrupt your teaching, is less likely to fuel a student who is acting out for attention, and saves your voice.

Individual Incentives

Use the following ways to recognize individual students who exhibit exemplary behavior:

- Brainstorm with students privileges or small prizes they would like to earn. Add the favorites to the blank Cool Coupons (page 114), and photocopy the reproducible on neon-colored card stock. Cut apart the coupons, and display them in a clear container. Keep a large supply of Cool Coupons available to reward students who are staying on task, helping a friend, or demonstrating appropriate behavior.

- When you want to reward students for accomplishments such as bringing back permission slips or homework on time, helping a friend, or being a good listener, give them a ticket. Have students write their name on the ticket and place it in a jar. Each week, draw a few winning tickets. Award small prizes (e.g., pencils, erasers, special markers) to the winners. Empty the jar each week or accumulate tickets all year.

- Gather pennies, nickels, dimes, and quarters. Have students make banks, wallets, or other containers to store the money. Tape an index card to the corner of each student's desk. Whenever you see a student setting a good example, add a tally mark to his or her "point card." Have students meet with you to trade in their points for money. Have students count up their points and tell you what coins they expect to get. Then, trade the points for money. Have students collect money for two weeks. Then, open the store (i.e., small items, each with a price). Invite students to make their purchases. Teach proper manners, patience while waiting in line, and the fact that we cannot always afford what we want. Explain how to save for larger purchases. After a few store openings, invite student volunteers to be the cashiers. Provide them with change and waist aprons or a cash drawer. Invite the volunteers to practice making the change and selling the items.

 Work with the class for the first few weeks reinforcing rules and procedures until routines are firmly established. Have students practice lining up and transitioning quietly. Be certain they know what to do with finished work and what to do when their work is done. The time spent at the beginning of the year pays off with time gained throughout the rest of the year.

Foster On-Target Behavior

- Create a prize box quickly and inexpensively from a shoe box covered with gift wrap or a plain plastic storage container. Fill the box or container with small inexpensive or free prizes (e.g., stickers, pencils, erasers, bookmarks, postcards, AAA Trip Tiks®). Look for items in the birthday party section of discount stores. Do not forget the free stickers you get in junk mail or from book clubs. Invite children to chose something from the prize box as a fun reward for behavior and effort above and beyond your expectations.

- Spray wooden nickels or plastic chips with gold paint. Give each student a juice can, and invite him or her to cover this "gold coin container" with colored contact paper. Supervise students as they use permanent markers to write their name on their can. Invite students to decorate their can with stickers and keep it at their desk or table or in their cubby. Then, as a class, list classroom privileges that can be earned with gold coins (e.g., line up first, choose book for teacher to read, receive stickers, read to another class, be errand person, eat lunch in the room). Look for students who follow classroom rules, use their time wisely, have a positive attitude, solve problems, or show respect for others, and reward them with a gold coin!

- For selected students who need additional positive reinforcement, photocopy on card stock the How Am I Doing? reproducible (page 115), and write the class schedule in the *Task* column. Sit down with each student, and show him or her the card. Explain that, at the end of each lesson or time slot, you will reward his or her appropriate behavior during each class period with a check, star, or sticker. Have the student tell you what that appropriate behavior will look like. Put the student in charge of taking responsibility for his or her own learning and not interfering with the learning of others. Challenge students to make progress each day. Tape a card to the corner of each student's desk. For the first week or so, check in with students after every activity. As they progress, you can check in a few times a day. Cross off class periods from the chart after two weeks if the student has consistently received stars and stickers during that time.

 Unlike adding stars by a student's name on a displayed chart, no one can tell whether a student is working on his or her fifth or tenth trip to the prize box—comparisons are too difficult to make.

Small-Group Incentive Programs

Using small groups to encourage on-target student behavior is smart teaching. Peers encourage each other to meet and exceed your expectations, and working together towards points or other rewards can bring a group together. Here are a few ways to reward groups who are working well together:

■ Draw a large box in the corner of your chalkboard or dry-erase board, and divide the box so that there is one section for each group in your class. Award points to the first few groups seated, attentive, and prepared for the next lesson following a transition. At the end of each week, give a reward to the three groups with the most points. For example, if you use raffle tickets, give each student in the group with the most points three tickets, each student in the group with the second-most points two tickets, and so on. If you award privileges, consider having a luncheon with the groups and bringing a dessert treat for each student.

■ Have each group generate a name (suggest themes at the start of each new grading period or unit) and write it on a large piece of construction or butcher paper. Invite the groups to decorate their banner, and then display the banners above the groups or on the walls. As students work together, award stickers or stamps to deserving groups on their banner. Count the stickers or stamps at the end of each week, and invite the group that earned the most stickers or stamps (for that week) to take a trip to the prize box, or offer some other suitable reward.

■ Photograph each group, and display the pictures on a bulletin board, each with a different color of 9" x 12" (23 cm x 30.5 cm) construction paper stapled beneath it. Add stickers or stamps to the corresponding paper as each group earns recognition. At the end of the week, award a small prize to the three groups with the most stamps or stickers. Change the paper at the end of each week.

Encourage independence by giving students options for activities when their work is finished (e.g., read a book, write a letter, work at a center). Keep their choices simple for the first few days of school, and then gradually increase their options until they have at least five or six different choices.

Foster On-Target Behavior

Whole-Class Incentive Programs

Rewarding a class for a job well done can help encourage individual students to do their best for the benefit of the class and brings the group together to work towards a common goal. Listed below are a few easy-to-implement systems for rewarding a class that is functioning well as a group. For each system, have the class agree in advance on the reward they are working towards (e.g., a pizza party, a movie in class).

■ Draw a ladder by the chalkboard. Each time the class exceeds expectations, move a footprint cutout one rung up the ladder. Award a prize when you place the footprint on the top rung. Alternatively, use a real ladder (which has fewer steps) and have the class earn five tally marks before you move the footprint each step.

■ Keep a jar in an easy-to-spot location of the classroom. Add a marble to the jar every time the class exceeds expectations. Award the class a prize when the jar is full.

■ Make a paper chain with a link for each point students must earn towards their prize. Hang the chain high enough to keep it safe, but low enough that students can reach it with your help. Every time the class deserves recognition for their behavior, have a student break the next link in the chain. When the last link is broken, give students their reward.

■ Create a scene representing the award on a bulletin board. At the bottom of the scene, add enough elements for each point the class must earn for the prize. Each time the class deserves recognition for their behavior, have a student move an element into the scene, until all the elements have been moved into the scene and the class earns the reward.

Teach Classroom Problem Solving

Help students solve their own conflicts by combining a little direct instruction with some smart environment choices. Here are a few of both:

■ Divide a common sequence of events into four or five steps, and list them on a chart or a large piece of butcher paper. Have the first step show a common classroom situation, such as *John, Rachel, and Susan took a ball out to recess.* Show the last step in the chart with a conflict like *"I'm never going to play with you again," said Susan as she ran away crying.* Ask students to consider what steps may have led up to the disagreement. Have them brainstorm the events to fill in the chart. After the chart is complete, discuss a better way the situation could have been handled.

■ Discuss empathy with students by asking them to verbalize their feelings. Encourage them to reflect on how their actions make others feel. Establish an understanding of cause and effect in relation to actions and the way those actions make others feel.

■ Work with students to generate a list of polite phrases to practice to avoid potential conflict. Examples might include

- *No, thank you.*
- *Please stop.*
- *Could we share that?*
- *May I play with you?*
- *I need help.*

■ Read aloud *Playground Problem Solvers* by Sandi Hill (Creative Teaching Press). Create a two-column chart titled *Problem* and *Solution* on large chart paper. Ask students to tell you the problems the monsters in the story had on the playground, and list their responses in the first column. Then, ask students to tell you how the monsters solved those problems, and write student responses in the second column. Post the chart on the wall for students to refer to as they work on how to become "Classroom Problem Solvers." Make a second two-column chart on large chart paper. Ask students to name problems that sometimes arise in the classroom, and record their responses in the first column. Discuss how a "problem solver" would handle a problem in the classroom, and record students' responses in the second column. Some of the same methods the monsters used in handling problems can be used in the classroom. Help students see that they are responsible for making smart choices when faced with a problem.

Problem	Solution
a friend picks computer first	take turns
a friend trips you	count to ten
a friend talks when you are working	ask him or her to stop
you step on a friend's foot	say you are sorry

Foster On-Target Behavior

- Create a "cool-down zone" in the classroom. Equip it with paper, pencils, and crayons. When students are involved in a conflict, have them go to the special location and write in a journal about their problem. This journal can be in writing or in picture form. Ask students to describe their problem and develop one solution they feel would resolve the issue. Give students five to ten minutes to work through their feelings. Meet with all individuals involved in the conflict, and mediate as they decide on an appropriate conclusion.

- Promote a positive classroom climate by instituting a "No Put-Down" rule. Encourage students to respect others with their language as well as their actions.

- Photocopy the Amazing Awards (page 116), cut apart the awards, and keep them close at hand. Make a point of giving awards to students on a regular basis. Encourage students to help friends, be honest, or stick to a job by recognizing their efforts.

 Young students need to move around or change activities often. This can be facilitated by simply putting scissors, glue, and sharp pencils in a place where students are encouraged to get out of their seats to get them. If all supplies are kept in students' desks, students do not have legitimate reasons to get up and move—something they need to do.

Track Growth

Each year your students will learn new academic and social skills, and you will need to describe this growth to them, to their parents, and to your administrators. Here are some terrific ideas for capturing their growth on paper so you can refer to it later when someone catches you in the hall with a question.

Use Anecdotal Notes

Set up a binder to file notes on behavior throughout the year. Have a section for each student. File several copies of the Kid Watch reproducible (page 117) in each student's section. Throughout the day, record on sticky notes academic and behavioral observations of students during activities. Jot the student's name and the activity at the top of each note. At the end of the day, transfer the sticky notes to the appropriate columns of the Kid Watch reproducible to help track growth and needs. Look for patterns in behavior (e.g., always responsible, frequently off task, eager to answer questions). Privately discuss needs for growth with individual students at recess or after school, and then look for this growth. Share your notes during parent/teacher conferences to support your observations. If behavior is an issue over time, photocopy the student's page at the end of each day and send it home for parents to read, sign, and return to school the next day.

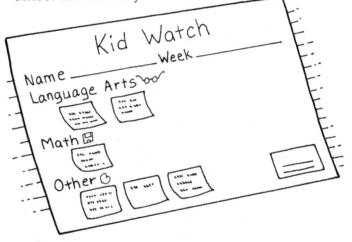

Create a File Box

Create a file box for 3" x 5" (7.5 cm x 12.5 cm) index cards with each student's name on a dividing tab. Place stacks of 3" x 5" cards and felt-tip pens in various locations around the room. Throughout the day, if a student shows improvement in a task or displays a work habit that needs improvement, jot down the student's name and a brief note. At the end of the day, date the cards and file them in the box. These provide a helpful resource during parent/teacher conferences or for reference during phone calls home.

 Always assume that a parent or administrator will be reading what you write about each student. Avoid subjective comments, especially negative ones (e.g., *ran with scissors today* instead of *is dangerous to self and others*, or *lice problem still not resolved* instead of *parent not washing hair*). Stick to the facts.

Create Portfolios

Portfolios provide physical evidence of students' ability to meet content standards and learning expectations. Label a legal-size file folder with each student's name, and store the folders in a location accessible to you and your students. Have students select pieces of their work to include in their portfolio. Periodically meet with each student to review the work in his or her portfolio and assess growth.

Teach Student Self-Assessment

Student self-assessment tools such as rubrics and journals are excellent ways of maintaining data on student growth. Try both of these tools:

- Class-generated rubrics are especially meaningful since the act of defining the learning goals is part of the process of defining the rubrics. Assign students a short activity in the content area for which you are generating a rubric. Then, use papers without names from previous years, or generate a high, medium, and low paper yourself. Do not use a paper from a current student. Invite students to discuss the differences in the papers and define the areas in which the papers excel or need work. Have students assign merit numbers to each definition. Guide the discussion to include the areas you will be assessing. For example, point out how clear handwriting makes the high paper easier to read. When the class has defined each level of the rubric (as many as five levels, as few as three levels), invite students to examine their own paper and use the rubric to assess their own work and that of two friends. Have them write why they felt they earned the rubric score they did and what they intend to do differently next time to improve their score (e.g., *I will use capital letters and periods the next time I write*).

- Journals give students time to reflect on various tasks. From time to time, write questions for students to elicit assessment information for specific standards. Periodically collect and read the journals, and then meet with students to discuss their entries.

Invite Parent Comments

Parental input can also be an important method of tracking student achievement. Periodically send home a checklist for parents to complete. Include questions such as

- *Does your child read at home?*

- *What strengths do you see in your child?*

- *In what one area do you feel your child needs to improve?*

- *What is one thing about your child that makes you proud?*

Build Community

Laughing and playing together is a vitally important part of learning together, and making the time to do so in a purposeful way builds a sense of community and teamwork. The following activities and ideas are geared towards creating a classroom that works and learns cooperatively.

Build the Community

Establish the fact that the class is a team from the first day of school by creating a themed room environment. On the first day, have the class vote on a class name. For the rest of the year, use this name. Students will take pride in their name and view themselves as a team. Examples of themes include the following:

- Ocean

  - Class names: Sea Stars, Awesome Orcas, Beach Buddies

  - Room environment: ocean borders, ocean-related pictures, real sea stars and shells on display, inflatable raft in the reading corner, picnic table for the listening center

- Rainbow

  - Class names: Rainbow City, Rainbow Friends, Rainbow Builders

  - Room environment: handprint rainbow wall display on blue butcher paper, sun around the clock

- Bear

  - Class names: Bear Buddies, Warm Fuzzy Crew, Bear Land, Great Grizzlies, Bear Junction, Bear Bonanza

  - Room environment: huge bear on the door holding a beehive with each student's name on it, teddy bears, cave made from butcher paper and wire

- Solar System

  - Class names: Space Station # (room number), Adventurous Astronauts, Rocket Launchers, Shining Stars

  - Room Environment: large rocket made out of boxes, cone covered with foil (students sit inside to read), astronaut and space posters, stars on ceiling

77

Recognize a Student of the Week

Celebrate your students by giving each one his or her own week. Call the students "Star of the Week," "VIP," or "Student of the Week." Then, try a combination of the following ideas for making each student feel important in your class:

- At the start of the week, invite the student to choose a few classmates to trace his or her body on butcher paper. Provide the students with art materials, and have them decorate the student's "body." Hang the finished art piece on the door of the classroom for the week.

- If you have an estimating jar, surprise box, or other learning tool that goes home with your students, give it to the student to take home at the beginning of the week. Have him or her return it at your usual sharing time.

- Invite the student to decorate the border of the class newsletter before you photocopy it to send home.

- Invite the student to arrange self-portraits and family photos on a bulletin board. At the end of the week, have the student give a presentation about the display he or she made.

- Have the student's classmates each write a letter describing his or her best attributes and the ways in which that student is valuable to the class. Write one yourself. Invite the student's parents to write one, too.

- Send home a photocopied set of the reproducibles on pages 118–122 in a folder or sealed envelope with each student. Write a letter to parents that gives a due date and explains the activity, and attach it to the front of the folder. Post the completed pages during each student's week, and then invite him or her to make and decorate a cover. Bind the pages and the cover into a completed book. This project serves multiple purposes: a family photo opportunity, a star of the week display, and individually bound books to save for Open House in the spring.

Create a Class Motto

Encourage students to list skills for student success. This list might include listen to others, cooperate, think critically, think creatively, set goals, communicate clearly, work independently, work cooperatively, solve problems, motivate self and others, and appreciate diversity. Invite the class to decide which ideas they want to include in their class motto. Ask small groups of students to illustrate each idea, and display their work between the titles *If you can ____ and ____, you can do anything!* Encourage the class to say the motto together daily.

If you can cooperate and work together, you can do anything!

Host a Class Mascot

Find a stuffed animal your students like. If you have a room theme, find a related animal to be your class mascot. Have the class name the mascot. Every day, choose a student to take the mascot home. Place any or all of the following materials into a backpack labeled with your school name and room number:

- stuffed animal

- fiction and nonfiction books related to the animal

- related story on tape

- tape player

- disposable camera

- journal

- instruction and suggested activities sheet

Take the backpack home first. The next morning say that you read the books, played with the animal, listened to the tape, wrote about your night in the journal (show the journal entry), and asked someone to take one picture of you with the animal. Read the journal entry. Tell students you will place the pictures in a photo album for the second round of home visits. Then, choose the first student to take home the backpack. Do not send it home on weekends (which doubles that students' time with the mascot and increases the chance the mascot may get lost).

79

Find the Mascot

Use the class mascot (see page 79) to help students familiarize themselves with the layout of the school and some of its support staff. Follow these steps for a fun activity:

1. Make sure the class mascot has been introduced and has a designated location as a home. Give the class mascot to a school helper (e.g., cafeteria employee, janitor, office assistant). Read aloud *Detective Dog and the Search for Cat* by Sandi Hill (Creative Teaching Press). Then, innocently ask a volunteer to bring the class mascot to the front of the room (do not reveal that you know the mascot is gone). When the student reports it missing, pretend to be upset and concerned. Work with students to devise a plan to find the mascot. Give each student a Wanted reproducible (page 123). Tell students to create a wanted poster for the class mascot, including a picture and important information to post around the school. This information should answer the following: What kind of animal is it? What color is it? What is its name? How big is it?

2. After a short break, tell the class they will search the school to find the mascot. Show students a school map. List on chart paper areas students will search. Assign a team of students to be the spokespeople at each area, and have them bring their wanted posters. Visit each location on the school map. Have the team assigned to that location show their wanted posters, give the information about the mascot, and ask the people at each place if they have seen the mascot. Before leaving each location, mark it off the list. After the mascot is found, return to the classroom and trace on the map the route of your search.

3. Reread *Detective Dog and the Search for Cat*. Post your school map, and trace with markers the path the class followed. For less fluent writers, have the following sentence frames on the board: *Was ___ (name of mascot)___ in the _(place name)_? No, but _(name of school helper)_ was in the _(place name)_.* Ask the class if the mascot was in each location they went to on the map. Model how they should respond, naming whom they met at that location and what they were doing. Invite more fluent writers to describe the search independently. Work together to create a class book titled *Looking for _(name of mascot)_*. If you use the sentence frames, print them on large sheets of construction or butcher paper and have students help you fill in the blanks. Have students work in small groups to illustrate each page.

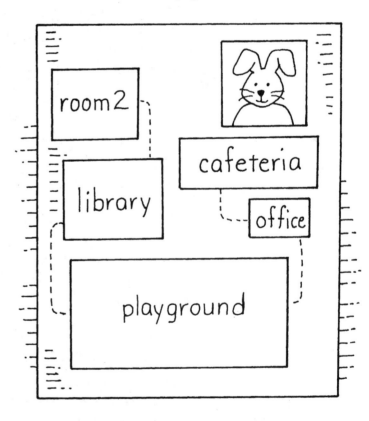

Celebrate Birthdays

Make a class set of birthday crowns or cupcake cards so you will have them at a moment's notice. Have each student use art supplies (e.g., glitter glue, sequins, dot paints) to decorate a crown. Make sure they write their name on their crown. Make a few extras for students who transfer into your class after the start of school. Store the crowns. When students celebrate their birthday, give them their crown to wear all day. Create a birthday bag with fun activities for the student to enjoy on his or her birthday. Some items include

- birthday books

- bubbles and bubble wands

- games

- birthday journal (to record what he or she did)

Create a large construction paper cupcake card for each student. Add paper candles to the top. On each student's birthday, have students sign the cupcake and write a group message for the birthday friend. Send it home with the student that day.

 At the beginning of the year, send home a note explaining procedures for birthdays in your class. Tell parents if birthday treats are acceptable or if you prefer a book donated to the class in the student's name.

81

Honor Lost Teeth

Make at least two class sets of little containers in which students take home lost teeth. Containers could be

- film canisters with tiny labels that say *I lost a tooth today!*

- plastic bags with *I lost a tooth today!* labels

- plastic tooth necklaces available from carnival stores or mail-order catalogs

Make a "Tooth Tote" to help students celebrate with their family. Include the following items in a backpack:

- lost-teeth stories (e.g., *The Lost Tooth Club* by Arden Johnson-Petrov, *Cousin Ruth's Tooth* by Amy MacDonald)

- "Tooth Fairy Tales"—a journal in which students record what they think the Tooth Fairy looks like or what the fairy will do with the tooth

- hand mirror so student can admire the new hole

Send home the Tooth Tote with students. Invite students to share their celebration the next day and read aloud their journal entry. Keep a "Tooth Tally" on your calendar. Have students add tally marks to represent lost teeth. Have students predict how many teeth the class will lose by the end of the year, and post the prediction. Revise the prediction when more teeth are lost.

Introduce Blankets and Other Warm Fuzzies

Read aloud *Owen* by Kevin Henkes. Invite students to predict how Owen and his family will solve his dilemma (i.e., he is not ready to give up his security blanket though the start of school is swiftly approaching). Then, read on to see how the characters come up with creative solutions. At the end of the story, give each student a small square piece of felt fabric. Many students will keep this "blanket" with them throughout the year.

Host a Back-to-School Night

Back-to-School Night goes by different names and is scheduled at various times from school district to school district, and sometimes even within a district. The overall objective of the night is to give parents an opportunity to learn what their children will be learning and doing that year, give them a chance to get to know you a little, and allow you to reach out to them. Some parents will come to Back-to-School Night and Open House (in the spring) and not set foot on school grounds any other time of the year. Back-to-School Night is your opportunity to get them involved in their child's learning at least by informing them of the activities that will take place in your classroom. If you can convince them to volunteer for field trips, read with their child every night, or publish your newsletter for you, all the better. The following tips and activities are written as if you will be addressing parents in your own classroom and are easily adapted for use by a group of teachers addressing an entire grade level.

Prepare for Back-to-School Night

Back-to-School Night may be the first time you meet your students' families. Make a list of what you want to tell your students' parents. (See page 84 for a sample list.) Prepare handouts ahead of time, and put them in a folder for each parent. These handouts should review everything you will cover in your Back-to-School Night presentation. Have students decorate the front of the folders, or glue a self-portrait of each student to the appropriate folder. (See pages 44, 45, 47, and 48 for ideas.) Include a table of contents at the front, and maintain a professional look to the packet. If you have a favorite handout that is a copy of a copy of a copy (and looks it), retype it and add updated artwork. Keep the masters in a file folder so you can use them again next year.

Create your own business cards on colored card stock, and laminate them. Include your name, school name, grade level, room number, and the school phone number (or a voice mail or home phone number, if you are comfortable with this). Stick a magnetic strip to the back of each card so parents can keep it on their refrigerator. Attach your business card to your Back-to-School Night parent information packet. It is a personal touch that parents appreciate.

Back-to-School Night Presentation Topics

As time permits, choose from the following topics for your Back-to-School Night presentation:

- curriculum for the first grading period (and the entire year, if you know it)

- field trips and related rules

- daily schedule

- school procedures (e.g., signing in at the office before you visit the classroom)

- brief description of the classroom rules and how you enforce them

- homework

- lunch procedures

- supplies

- labels for anything child brings to school

- book orders

- special events for the year

- dismissal procedure/school rules related to going home

- guidelines for birthday celebrations

- enrichment classes (e.g., computers, foreign languages, music, art)

- how parents can

  - volunteer in the classroom

  - help their child become an independent/self-motivated learner (show How Parents Help reproducibles, pages 124–125)

  - teach responsibility at home

  - read at home

  - build independent/self-motivated students

  - foster a love of learning (show School Gifts reproducible, page 126)

  - be a learning cheerleader (show What Did You Do at School Today? reproducible, page 127)

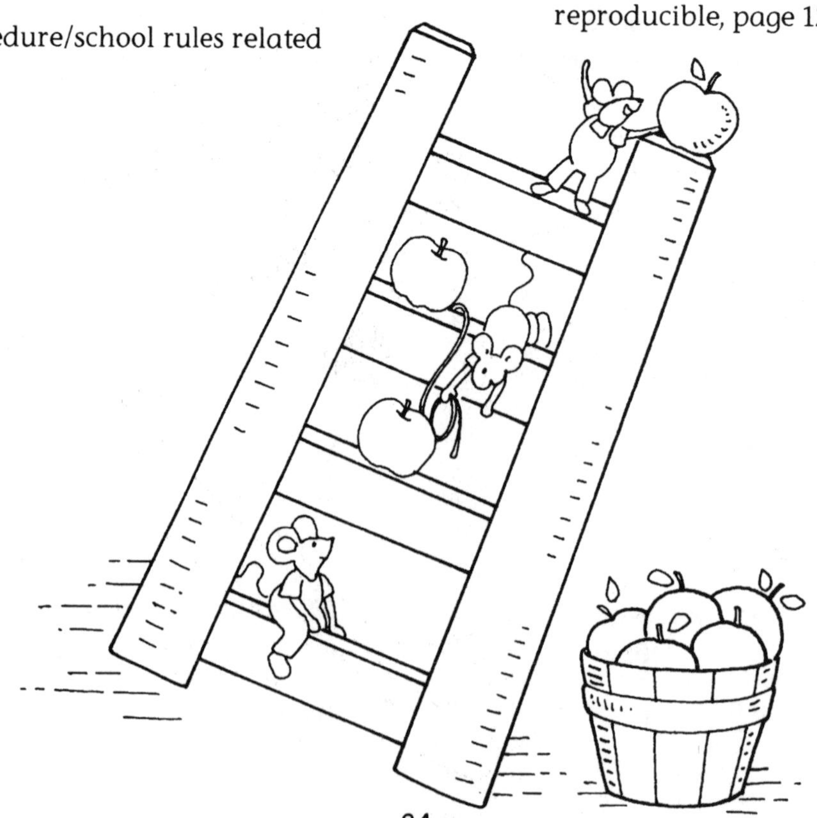

The Back-to-School Night Parent Packet

Include in your Back-to-School Night parent packet any information that involves parents in their child's education, such as

- How Parents Help reproducibles (pages 124–125)

- School Gifts reproducible (page 126)

- What Did You Do at School Today? reproducible (page 127)

- copy of the report card

- list of goals related to the report card

- brief outline of your curriculum for the year

- daily schedule

- brief description of the classroom rules and how you enforce them

- information about book orders

- school calendar

- map of the school

- list of upcoming field trips

- student medical release forms

- parent driver insurance forms (or other forms required for parents who volunteer to drive for field trips, if your school does not provide busses for field trips)

- field-trip permission slips (if you already scheduled your trips)

- recommended book list for students

- sample of the handwriting style guide your school uses

- list of words their child should be able to read

85

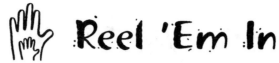

Reel 'Em In

Have an adult classroom volunteer make a videotape of each student saying his or her full name, age, likes and dislikes, and hopes and dreams for the year. Use an accurate height chart as the background. Have students rehearse what they will say once or twice before they are taped. Play the finished tape while parents are arriving and looking around the room on Back-to-School Night. At the end of the year, repeat this activity at the end of the same tape. Invite students to compare how much they grew by having them look at the height chart and note the differences in their voices, mannerisms, and dreams. The completed tape is also fun to play back for students in the last half-hour of the school year.

Win at Back-to-School Night

Encourage parental participation in Back-to-School Night by holding a raffle. Have each student write his or her name on a specially designed piece of paper or ticket. Tell students to encourage a family member to attend Back-to-School Night to enter their ticket in your lottery. Draw one name at the end of the evening, and give that person a prize such as the following to take home for the student: a collection of school supplies, a certificate for lunch with the teacher or principal, or a book.

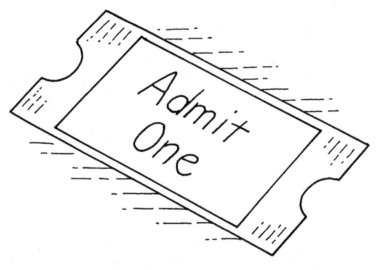

The key to a successful Back-to-School Night is to stay upbeat and positive. Parents are nervous, too. Make them glad they came and they'll come back. Remember that first impressions last! Remember to be optimistic and excited; shake hands; smile; and be professional, friendly, and enthusiastic!

Keep It Visual

Tell parents in advance that you will be showing color slides of their children at Back-to-School Night and they will be more likely to show up. Obtain a slide projector and slide film. Take candid pictures of your students throughout the day as they complete routine tasks (e.g., journal writing, working at centers, completing classroom jobs, adding words to a word wall or word bank, earning rewards for good behavior, packing up at the end of the day). Keep track of who is in each picture to ensure that every student is included in the slide show. Take one or two rolls of pictures, more if you are uncertain about the lighting. Have your slides developed at least one week in advance. Organize them in the order of your daily schedule, put them in the projector, and practice your presentation with them. Use the slides to guide your presentation and highlight what you are saying. Speak as you show the pictures. Parents will enjoy the photos, and you will feel more relaxed! Save the slides for a future raffle, or give them away to interested parents. If you cannot find a slide projector, make color transparencies of photos. Add black-and-white transparencies of old newsletters, common forms parents can expect to see, rewards or coupons their children may earn, and you have a complete and satisfying presentation.

Host a Back-to-School Night

Avoid Chaos

Use signs and instruction sheets to create stations on tables or desks. Write the information you display on card stock, but do not laminate anything. You may make changes from year to year, and what seems set in stone this year, may not be next year. Give each parent a checklist of all stations and a pencil. Invite parents to go to each station, follow any instructions, and check off that station on their list. Parents will feel confident that they have received all of your information, and you will feel organized and in control. Smile and enjoy!

Stations might include

- copies of each literature book you will be reading

- math manipulatives and samples of concepts you teach with them

- science manipulatives

- examples of papers in various stages of the writing process

- opportunities for parent involvement (see pages 12–15)

- parent/teacher conference sign-up sheet

- sign-up sheet for field-trip transportation and related parent forms

Don't Worry, Be Happy

Keep the following tips in mind for a Back-to-School Night free from worries:

- Do not worry about making a good first impression. Focus on being enthusiastic, positive, and friendly and you will be a big hit!

- Do not worry about your classroom being perfect. Post one example of each student's work and you are covered.

- Do not worry about having the entire year mapped out. Share student goals for the first grading period and keep them simple.

- Do not worry about giving all of the details of how discipline problems will be handled. Focus on the positive way you approach teaching and how it minimizes problem situations.

- Do not worry. If you stay focused on sharing with the parents that their children are your top priority and that by working together you can make it a great year for their kids, then everybody will be happy!

Look to the Finish Line

At the end of the year, you will barely remember how small and young your students seemed when you met them on the first day of school. You will all have come a long way (no matter how many times you may have made the school-year journey before), and you should honor that growth. Students will grow by inches and pounds and be astonished by the math, reading, and writing skills they have gained. Use the following easy-to-implement activities at the beginning of the year, and encourage students to reflect on all their changes at the end of the year.

Record Reading Development

Send a letter to parents asking them to each donate a blank videotape. Label each video-tape with the student's name. Store the labeled videos in a box. These will become your students' personal reading videos, documenting their reading development. When you start recording will depend on your grade level, students, and when a parent volunteer is available. Pick a parent with a positive attitude. Show the parent volunteer how to operate the video camera. Explain to the volunteer that you want each student to read aloud a book of his or her choice while being taped at least once each month. Have the parent organize the videos to keep track of who has read recently and who is next. Provide the parent volunteer and student with a quiet room or have them go outside. Have the volunteer state the date, have the student read a familiar book uninterrupted, send the student back into the classroom, and then repeat the process with another student. At the end of the year, encourage students to gift wrap their video and give it to their parents with a card that says *I am a reader!*

89

Begin an End-of-the-Year Memory Book

If you take lots of photos throughout the year, why not make them into individual memory books for your students? To begin this project, you will need to create a file for each student (e.g., an index-card box with a section for each student, a labeled envelope for each student, a clear plastic bag for each student, a file folder for each student contained in an expandable folder). Place a few developed pictures in each student's file. When developing film, get double or triple prints because many photos will have more than one student. Before you put the memory books together, list the activities and places where the photos were taken. Then, use a computer to make a heading for each place or event (e.g., *At the Pumpkin Patch, Our Thanksgiving Feast*). Print the headings on colorful paper, and attach the pictures with a glue stick. Have more advanced students help assemble their own books and write titles and captions. For less advanced students, enlist a few parents to help. Decorate the pages with stickers and die-cut shapes to add pizzazz. These books will also need covers. For the cover you can

- print each student's name, grade, and school year, and then add his or her picture from the first day of school

- have students decorate their own construction paper cover

- photocopy the school logo on colored card stock

Laminate the front and back cover for durability. Use a bookbinding machine to bind the completed pages together. Your students will be thrilled to have a memory book of their class and all the great things they did throughout the year. Ask students to bring a few books back the following year so you can display them for Back-to-School Night.

Begin an End-of-the-Year Class Book

Make a class book for the next year's class. Brainstorm with students the activities, projects, and field trips your class has participated in. Next, have each student complete the sentence frame *In _____ grade, I _____*. Type each student's sentence, and have him or her illustrate it. Bind the books, add a class picture to the cover, and they are ready for next year. When school begins the following year, you can read the book to your class to tell them all about the fun and fabulous things they will be doing.

Make a Time Capsule

For each student, fill a 9¹/₂" x 12¹/₂" (24 cm x 31.5 cm) envelope with several samples of work from the first few weeks of school. These are your "time capsules." Have students glue a photo of themselves in the center of the flower on the Watch Me Bloom reproducible (page 128), and then have students glue the reproducible to their envelope. On Back-to-School Night, give each envelope to the appropriate parents. Encourage parents to examine their child's work and write a short note to their child. Explain to parents that their child will not read the note until spring at an end-of-the-year party. Ask parents to seal the time capsules. On the following school day, have the class use wrapping paper to wrap the time capsules together in one box. Write *Do not open until (date of end-of-the-year party)* on the box. Put the box on a high shelf until the date you have chosen. On that day, remove the box from the shelf and invite the class to open it. Invite students and their families to compare the work done when school started to the work at the end of the year. Students and parents will see the progress that the class has made.

Suggested contents for time capsules include
- photograph of the student.

- sample of the student's printing.

- sample of the student's drawing.

- cassette of the student reading.

- picture of his or her family drawn by student.

- end-of-the-year math test. (Have student take the test in September for the time capsule and again at the end of the school year for comparison.)

- index card with the student's height and weight.

91

Daily Schedule

Time	Monday	Tuesday	Wednesday	Thursday	Friday

Volunteer Guidelines

Thank you so much for volunteering in the classroom. You are now a valued part of our school family. I know your time in our classroom will be very rewarding for you, and it will be a tremendous help to us.

Please keep a few things in mind when you are working with the students.

- Please check in with the front office.

- Be positive with the students and with the work that they do. Maintain realistic standards for their work.

- Feel free to help a student. However, we encourage students to do all the work. Students learn by experimenting . . . so let them do their work if at all possible. Ask them first, "What do you think you should do?"

- Remember to keep what happens in the classroom in the room. Please don't discuss the lives or learning of the students you assist with other students or adults who are not in the classroom. On the other hand, if you have a concern, please feel free to bring it to my attention immediately.

- Please remember to be on time. If you are unable to come at your scheduled time, please call the office, send a note, or try calling someone else on the volunteer list to see if he or she can substitute for you. We do depend on you.

- Try to stay as professional as possible. Please keep in mind that we are always role models for the students.

- Have fun with the students and enjoy yourself!

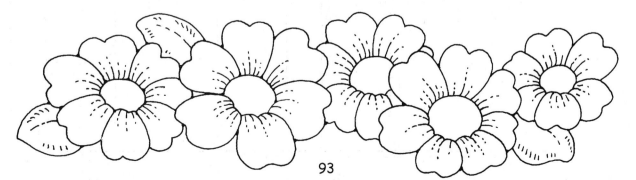

Lists

Survival
List

Back to School • K–3 © 2000 Creative Teaching Press

Book Order Parent Letter

Dear Parents,

Attached is the book order for the month of _____. Here are three
great books you might consider for your child's collection this month.

1.

2.

3.

Please send exact change or a check made payable to _____,
along with the completed order form in an envelope. Print your child's name and
room number on the order form. Turn in all orders no later than _____
if you wish to order books this month.

Thank you,

Check when done:
☐ I have marked the books I wish to order.
☐ Child's name is on the order form.
☐ Exact change or a check is in the envelope.

Contact

Student_____ Birthdate_____

Mailing Address _____

Parents/Guardians _____

Best Times to Call _____

Home Phone _____ Work Phone _____

Emergency Contact _____ Phone _____

Special Information _____

Date _____ Who Contacted _____

How: Phone   Note w/ Child   Mail   In Person

Summary _____

_____

_____

_____

Date _____ Who Contacted _____

How: Phone   Note w/ Child   Mail   In Person

Summary _____

_____

_____

_____

Date _____ Who Contacted _____

How: Phone   Note w/ Child   Mail   In Person

Summary _____

_____

_____

_____

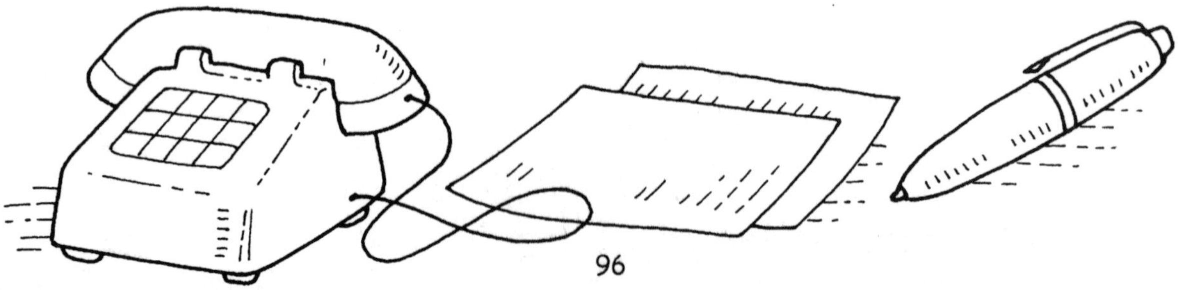

Back to School • K–3 © 2000 Creative Teaching Press

School Supply Checklist

Name	Supplies	crayons	glue	tissue	pencils	ruler	eraser	markers				

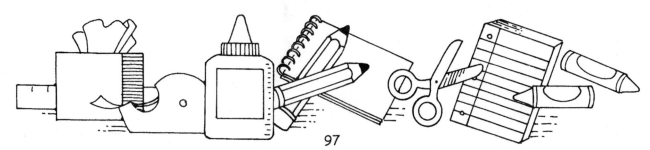

I Am Special

Frame Me

Can Do

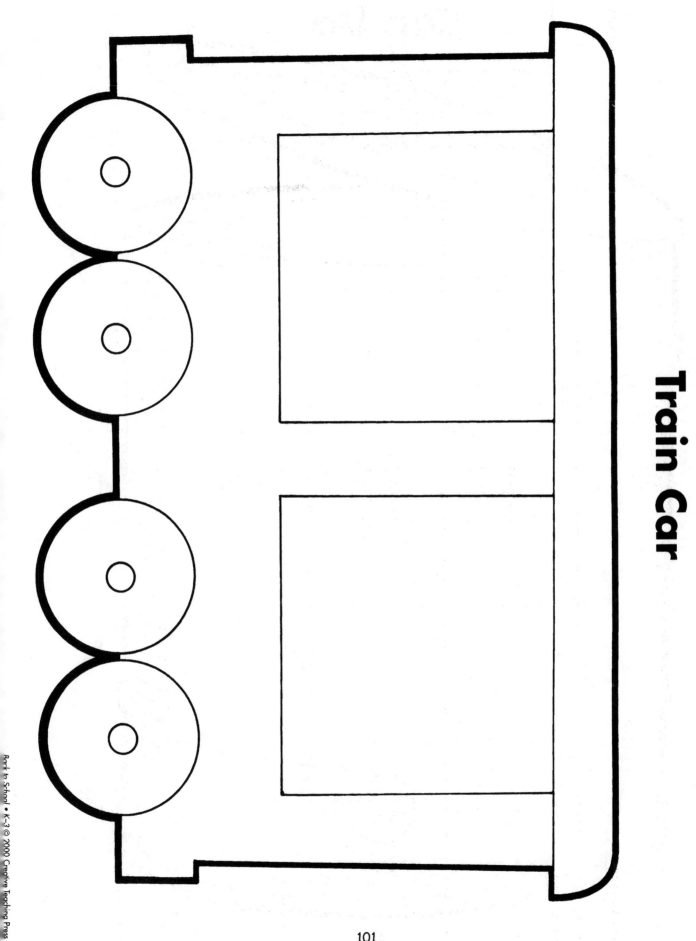

Train Car

Train Engine

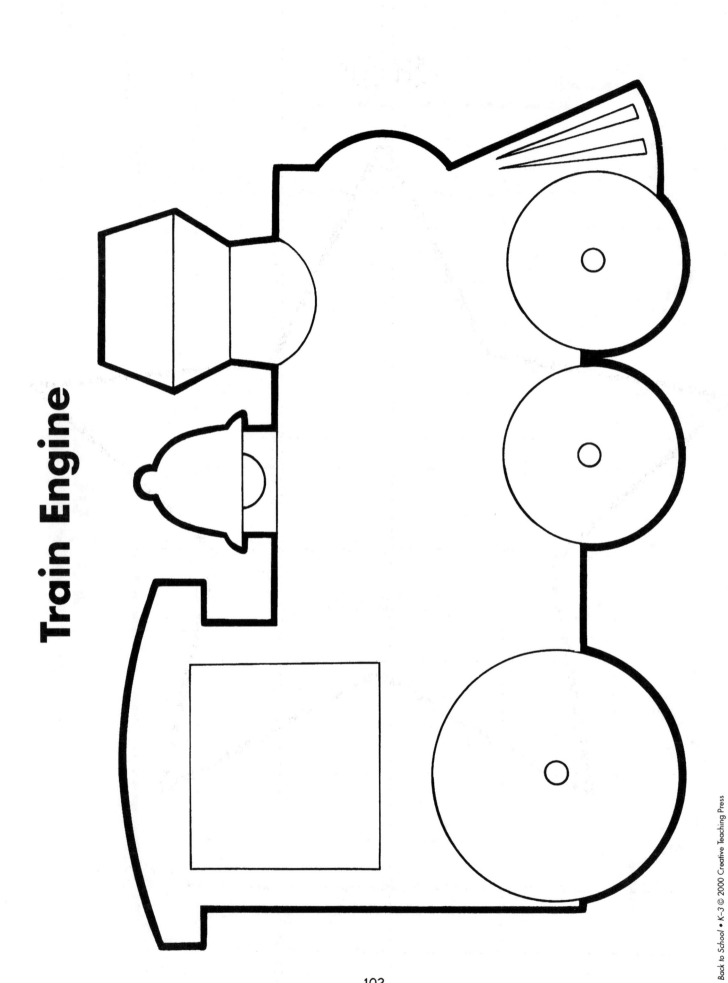

Back to School • K-3 © 2000 Creative Teaching Press

Star

_____ is good at

_____ .

Apples

Name_____ Date _____

Just like Me

	Me		Just like Me

Me   Just like Me

Eye Color _____   _____

Hair Color_____   _____

Favorite Sport_____   _____

Favorite Season _____   _____

Friends

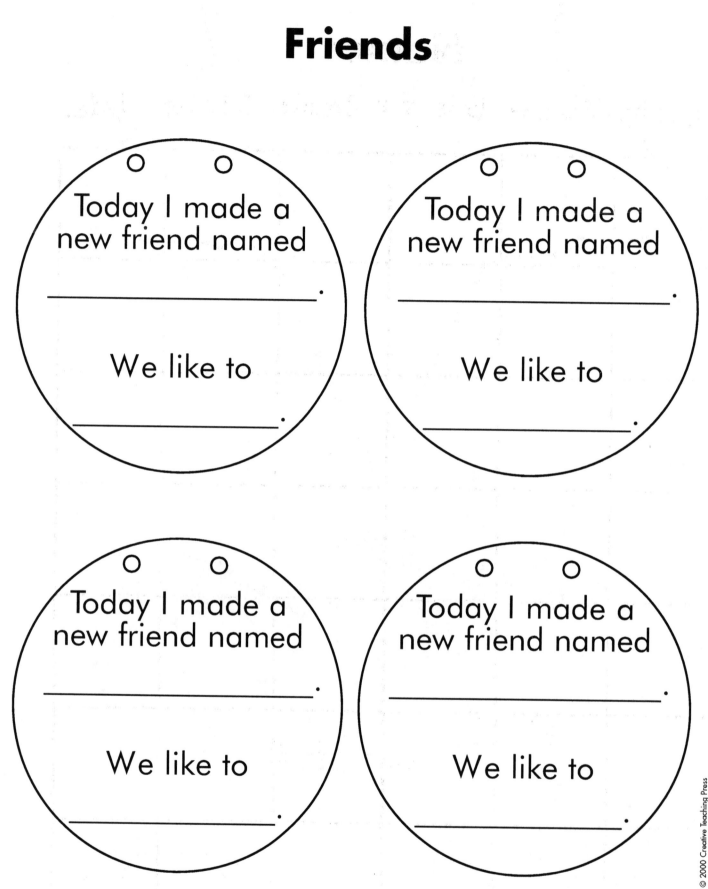

Today I made a
new friend named

_____.

We like to

_____.

Today I made a
new friend named

_____.

We like to

_____.

Today I made a
new friend named

_____.

We like to

_____.

Today I made a
new friend named

_____.

We like to

_____.

Back to School • K–3 © 2000 Creative Teaching Press

Names

A is for Albert. B is for Bonnie. C is for Clyde.

Name _____

B	I	N	G	O

Transportation

Child's Name _____

Please write how your child will
get home each day.

Monday _____

Tuesday _____

Wednesday _____

Thursday _____

Friday _____

Parent Signature _____

Child's Name _____

Please write how your child will
get home each day.

Monday _____

Tuesday _____

Wednesday _____

Thursday _____

Friday _____

Parent Signature _____

Back to School • K–3 © 2000 Creative Teaching Press

Lunchtime

No Homework Card

Date

No Homework Card

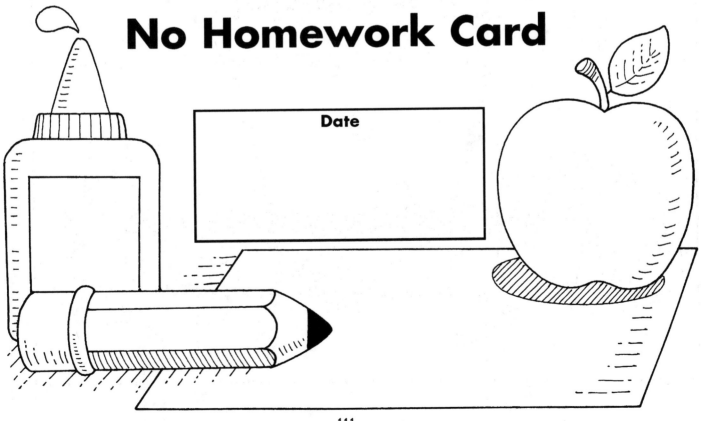

Date

Coaches' Contract

As the parent and coach, I promise to

- make reading fun

- read with my child every night

- praise continuously

- encourage proper care of the books my child brings home

- accept responsibility for the replacement of lost or damaged books

I have read the terms of the Coaches' Contract and want my child to be able to bring books home each night. I gladly accept the terms of the contract and look forward to being a great coach for my child.

Child's Signature _____

Parent Signature _____

Back to School • K–3 © 2000 Creative Teaching Press

Name _____

Book Log

Date	Book Title	Page #

Cool Coupons

First in Line

Free Sticker

Teacher's Helper for a Day

Read to My Friend

Name _____

How Am I Doing?

Task	Mon.	Tue.	Wed.	Thurs.	Fri.

Amazing Awards

I Did It Myself!

Presented to _____

By _____

For _____

Certificate of Excellence

_____

To _____

From _____

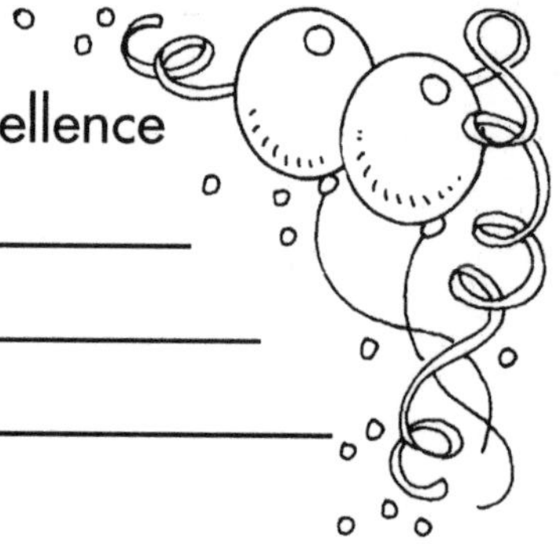

Friendship

_____

_____

Love _____

You'll always be a friend to me.

Achievement

_____

To _____

From _____

Leadership

_____

To _____

From _____

Honesty

_____

To _____

From _____

Positive Attitude

_____

To _____

From _____

Perseverance

_____

To _____

From _____

Kid Watch

Name _____   Week beginning _____

Language Arts

Math

Other

Comments

Parent Signature _____

Teacher Signature _____

This Is Me.

I am special.

My name is _____.

My hair is _____.

My eyes are _____.

I weigh _____.

I am _____ tall.

My nose is _____ long.

My smile is _____ wide.

Back to School • K–3 © 2000 Creative Teaching Press

Families Are Forever!

These are the members of my family: _____

_____.

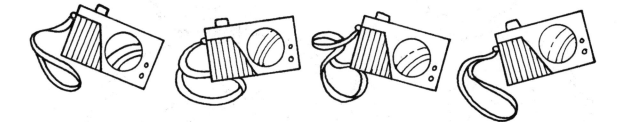

I Like To

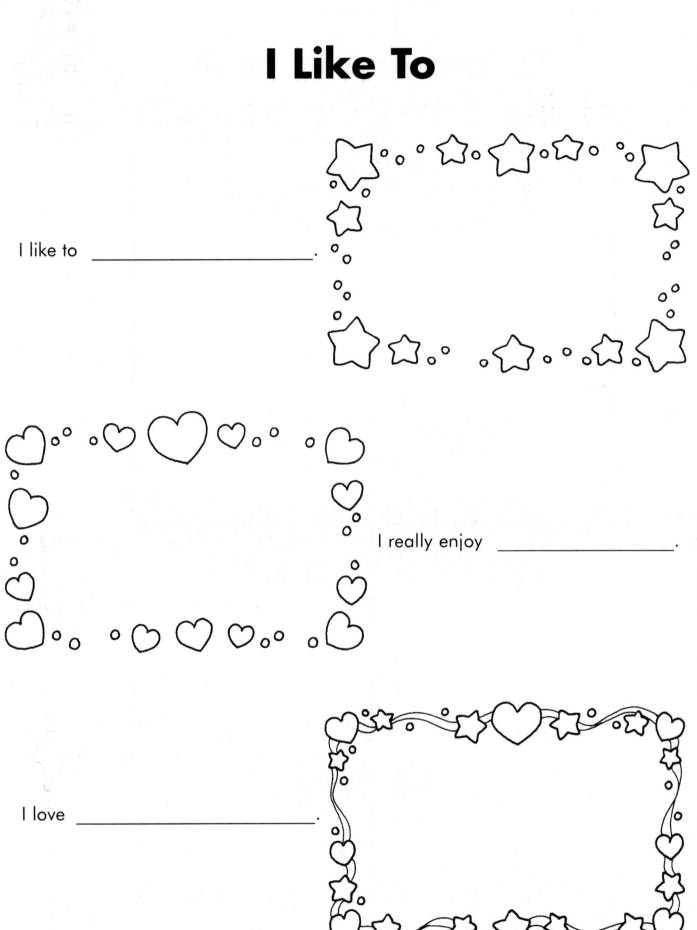

I like to _____.

I really enjoy _____.

I love _____.

These Are a Few of My Favorite Friends!

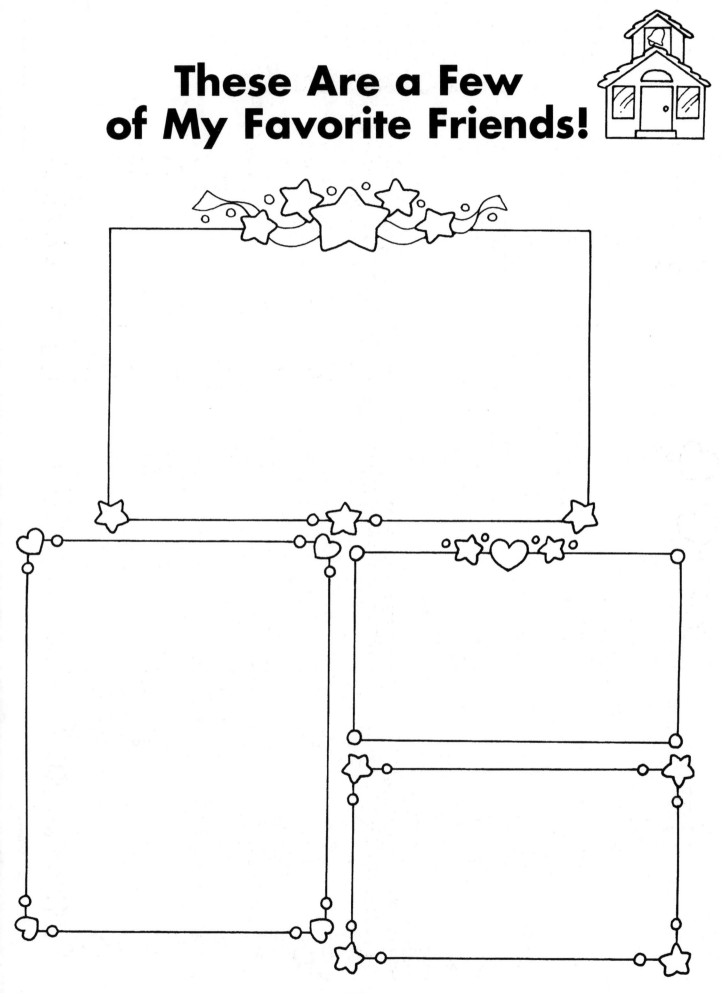

All about Me

My favorite story is _____.

My favorite outside activity is _____.

My favorite toy is _____.

My favorite song is _____.

My favorite place to visit is _____.

First thing in the morning, I like to _____.

Late at night, I like to _____.

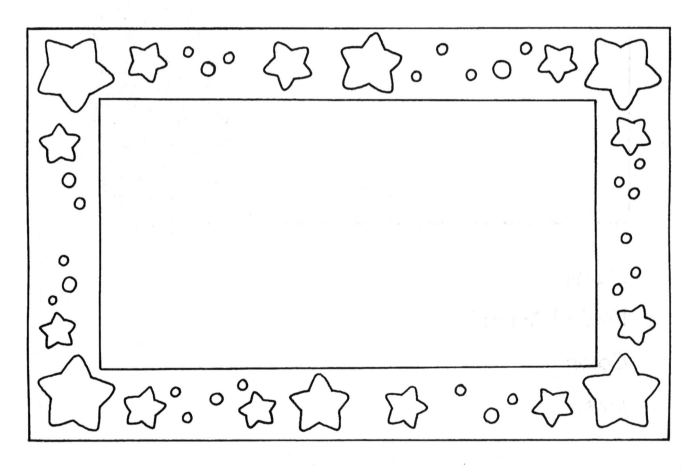

Here is my pet.

Its name is _____.

Wanted

Name:

Kind of Animal:

Color:

Size:

How Parents Help

Many things that you do at home on a daily basis will help your children the most. The activities described below benefit all children.

1. Set aside a special reading time. Tell your child you look forward to and enjoy your reading time together. Children who are read to—read.

2. Listen to your child. Oral language experience is also a foundation for literacy.

3. Talk to your child.

4. Make time to play with your child.

5. Solve problems with your child, instead of for him or her.

6. Have your child count everything and anything.

7. Write stories out as your child dictates them. Children love to see their ideas in print.

8. Praise your child whenever possible.

9. Talk with your child about school and everyday events.

10. Supervise homework. Give your child a quiet place to work, and check that assignments are completed.

11. Encourage exercise and good nutrition.

12. Encourage your child to write.

13. Broaden your child's horizons by taking him or her to parks, museums, libraries, zoos, and historical sites. All these places offer fun learning experiences.

14. Tell your child education is important, and encourage him or her to do well in school.

15. Children do not know intuitively how to behave; kindly but firmly teach your child.

16. Help your child get a library card from the public library. Take your child to the library as often as possible.

17. Help your child pick out interesting books to read.

18. Talk to your child about subjects that interest him or her.

19. Give your child his or her own place to keep books.

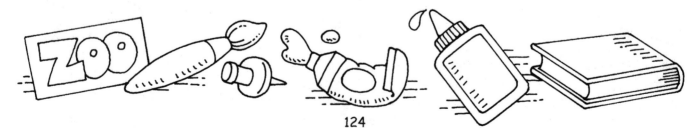

How Parents Help

20. Write notes to your child. Leave them to be found in special places—under pillows, in lunches, or in favorite books.

21. Encourage your child to keep a scrapbook about a subject that interests him or her (e.g., stamps, dogs, birds, trucks, photos of family activities).

22. Limit your child's television watching. Turn the television on for a specific show, and turn it off immediately after the show is over.

23. Read and discuss schoolwork with your child.

24. Provide materials for creative projects (e.g., crayons, pencils, paper, paint, scissors).

25. Give your child a calendar to write down special events and mark off each day.

26. Help your child make a telephone directory with the names and telephone numbers of his or her friends.

27. Ask your child to write or dictate a sentence or two for letters you write to faraway relatives.

28. Give your child specific duties at home to perform on a regular basis.

29. Invite your child to help you prepare dinner.

30. Subscribe to a children's magazine in your child's name.

31. Bring books for your child to read in the car.

32. Look up words in the dictionary with your child.

33. Encourage your child to show his or her schoolwork to your friends and relatives.

34. When traveling, read road signs with your child. Discuss what they mean.

35. Show your child how to use a yardstick, ruler, or tape measure to measure things around the house.

36. Give your child a special place to keep items he or she must regularly take to school.

37. Show your child how to tell time.

38. Hug your child daily.

School Gifts

Gift of Valuing Others—All children are important, and their opinions matter. We may be different, but everyone is special and unique.

Gift of Love of Learning—Children are excited with tasks from tying a friend's shoe to publishing their own book. They have a special capacity for absorbing great amounts of information.

Gift of Discovery—Children are challenged to discover new and different things in the world around them and to develop an interest in finding out the "why" in day-to-day occurrences.

Gift of Success—Every child receives the gift of success. When you are a little better today than you were the day before you are successful. Your child learns that he or she is good enough, and smart enough and people do like him or her.

Gift of Fun—Learning is fun, regardless of the subject area: math, reading, writing, or science. Discovering solutions to problems and adding to our knowledge makes a fun, academic year.

Back to School • K-3 © 2000 Creative Teaching Press

What Did You Do at School Today?

Every day parents ask their children what they did at school. Every day students answer, "Oh, nothing." Try asking these specific questions to get real answers.

What was something nice you said to a friend today?

What did you do in math?

What good book did your teacher read to you today?

Who did you play with today?

What did you write about today?

What was your favorite part of the day?

How are you going to make tomorrow even better?

What centers did you go to?

Who did you sit beside at lunch?

What did you learn in science?

Watch Me Bloom

Lots of green grass,

Lots of blue sea,

Many people,

Only one me!

Back to School • K–3 © 2000 Creative Teaching Press